WORDS All Around!

Phoenix International Publications, Inc.

we make books come alive®

Chicago • London • New York • Hamburg • Mexico City • Paris • Sydney

Puzzle Constructors: Cihan Altay, Myles Callum, Don Cook, Harvey Estes, David Millar, Michael Moreci, Alan Olschwang, Stephen Ryder, Pete Sarjeant, Fraser Simpson, Wayne Robert Williams

Illustrators: Erin Burke, Jen Torche

Contributing Writers: Holli Fort, Claire Winslow, and Rachel Halpern

© 2019 Merriam-Webster, Incorporated. Merriam-Webster and the bull's-eye design are registered trademarks of Merriam-Webster, Incorporated, and are used under license.

This publication may not be reproduced in whole or in part by any means whatsoever without written permission from the copyright owners. Permission is never granted for commercial purposes.

Published by Phoenix International Publications, Inc.
8501 West Higgins Road   59 Gloucester Place
Chicago, Illinois 60631   London W1U 8JJ

www.pikidsmedia.com

p i kids and *we make books come alive* are trademarks of Phoenix International Publications, Inc., and are registered in the United States.

ISBN: 978-1-5037-4577-3

Manufactured in China.

8 7 6 5 4 3 2 1

LET THE GECKOS BE YOUR GUIDES

Welcome to *Merriam-Webster Kids: Words All Around!* You'll find tons of different word puzzles, including One Up, Crunched Letters, Tile Tie-Ins, and so many more.

Your guides on this puzzling journey will be three gecko friends: Gene, Gina, and Gus. You'll encounter these reptiles throughout the book, and wherever they appear, you'll find a tip or trick to help you along, or a fun fact about words and dictionaries. You'll also want to keep an eye peeled for Lizard Linguistics, where you'll find tantalizing tidbits about puzzles and language.

Speaking of language, there's one important thing to note about these puzzles: we're not trying to trip you up, so all of the words used in the puzzles are ones that you can find in a Merriam-Webster dictionary. Maybe keep one close by in order to keep transforming those tiles into words. Leafing through a dictionary can really get your language juices going, so don't be scared to thumb through its pages from time to time.

Gene

> **linguistics** \liŋ-ˈgwis-tiks\ *noun* : the study of human speech including the nature, structure, and development of language

If you want to get a "geckologically sound" base for jumping into these puzzles, try following these handy tips:

Gina

Get the Lay of the Land
First things first: make sure you read the directions, so you know what you're getting into and can avoid sticky situations. For example, for some of these puzzles, it doesn't matter in what order you solve the clues, but for others, you have to start in a particular place (say, at the bottom) and build on the clues to work your way to the end. Other puzzles may have word pairs that are similar or opposite—you'll never know unless you pay attention to the directions!

Shoot for the Stars
You'll notice that every puzzle has a star icon. The number of stars—one, two, or three—tells you how hard a puzzle will be. You may want to start with a one-star puzzle, and then work your way up to completing the three-star puzzles. But remember, everyone is different. You may find that a certain kind of three-star puzzle is a snap, but a one-star puzzle holds you up for days.

Change the Pattern
If you get stuck, try thinking of the puzzle in a different way. For puzzles with jumbled letters, try writing down the letters in a random pattern on the page, instead of in a straight line. That may help you visualize possible connections in a different way. Even a

simple change in the way you're looking at the puzzle can make the solution become clearer.

Sticky Situations

If you get stuck on a puzzle, there are some simple things you can do to help get unstuck. If the puzzle is one where answers build on each other, step back and make sure that your answers to all the previous clues are correct. One wrong step along the way can cause problems later. If the puzzle is one that doesn't have to be solved in order, go ahead and fill in the easiest answers first, and use them to help you figure out the harder answers. And if all else fails, take a break and come back to it later. Switch to a different puzzle for a little while, and when you come back, you may have a new perspective.

Gus

The puzzles in *Merriam-Webster Kids: Words All Around!* are designed to keep you on your (very sticky) toes, and just as important, to make sure you have fun in the process. So slither on in, pick your puzzle, and get started!

Words All Around!

Level ★ ★

ONE UP

Use the three tiles at the bottom of the page to solve the bottom clue. Once you do that, move up the page, solving each clue as you go. Carry all the letters used from one clue to the next, rearranging them in the empty spaces.

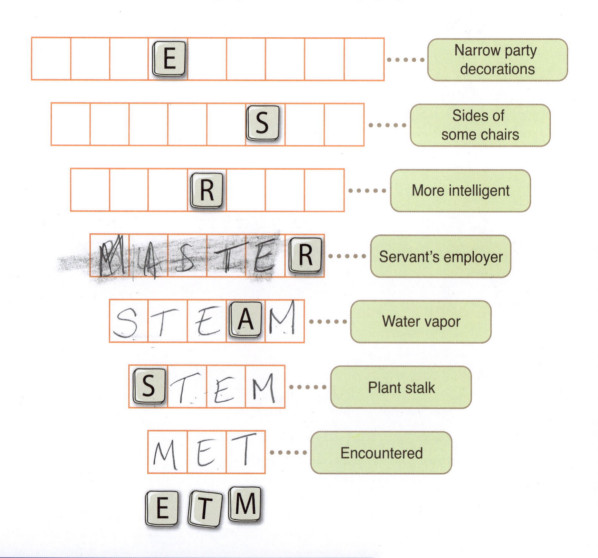

vapor \\'vā-pər\\ *noun* : a substance in the form of a gas

Answer on page 171.

Level ⭐ **Words All Around!**

ADD-A-LETTER

Rearrange the tiles from each word, adding one new tile from the bottom in order to form the name of an animal in the empty boxes. Each tile from the bottom of the page is used only once.

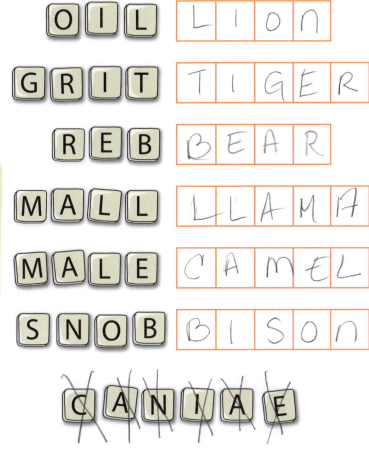

Given	Answer
OIL	LION
GRIT	TIGER
REB	BEAR
MALL	LLAMA
MALE	CAMEL
SNOB	BISON

Remaining tiles: ~~C~~ ~~A~~ ~~N~~ ~~I~~ ~~A~~ ~~E~~

What noise does a bee make? A bird? A mouse? "Buzz," "chirp," and "squeak" are all examples of "onomatopoeia," which is when the name of the word represents the sound it makes.

Words All Around!

WORD SWATTER

Create eight common words using three letters each from the word below. Letters will be used more than once to form all the words, but only once per word.

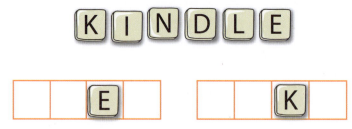

Merriam-Webster's biggest dictionary lists more than 476,000 words and weighs over ten pounds!

Lizard Linguistics

The most commonly used word in the English language is "the." You have to get all the way to number 50 before you find "me"!

Answer on page 171.

Level ★ ★ ★ Words All Around!

CROSSED OUT

Use the given tiles to spell a pair of related words that meet at the tile that has already been placed.

Level ★ ★ ★

SHUFFLE BOARD

Rearrange each of the letters in the tile groups below to form words. Place the new words into the grid. One letter has already been placed.

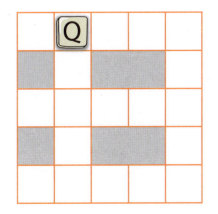

Answers on page 171.

Words All Around! Level

DROP LETTERS

Use all three letter tiles to create four-letter words below. Each tile will be used once per word.

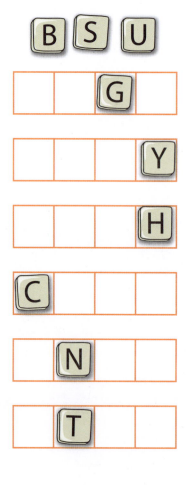

Level  Words All Around!

LETTER GRIDLOCK

Use the given tiles to complete the grid with words reading across and down. Use the clues, which are in a random order, to help discover the missing words.

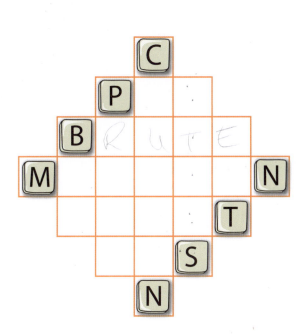

CLUES
- Uncovers
- Took a seat
- Straps to a horse's bridle
- Sack
- Really big guy
- Miles ___ hour
- France's capital
- Auntie, to mom
- Alien from the fourth planet
- Absolutely sure

bridle \brī-dᵊl \ *noun* : a device for controlling a horse made up of a set of straps enclosing the head, a bit, and a pair of reins

Answer on page 171.

Words All Around! Level

COME TOGETHER

Place each of the tile sets into the empty spaces below to create three nine-letter countries. Each tile set is used only once.

GUA GAP EZU

VEN ARA ORE

SIN NIC ELA

Think of some countries that you know, and see if any of the letters match.

country \ˈkən-trē\ *noun* : a land lived in by a people with a common government

Answer on page 172.

Level ★ ★ Words All Around!

THEME PARK

This "ride" has a theme, but we can't tell you what it is. Place all the words in the boxes below. Then read the word created in the outlined boxes, from top to bottom, to reveal the theme.

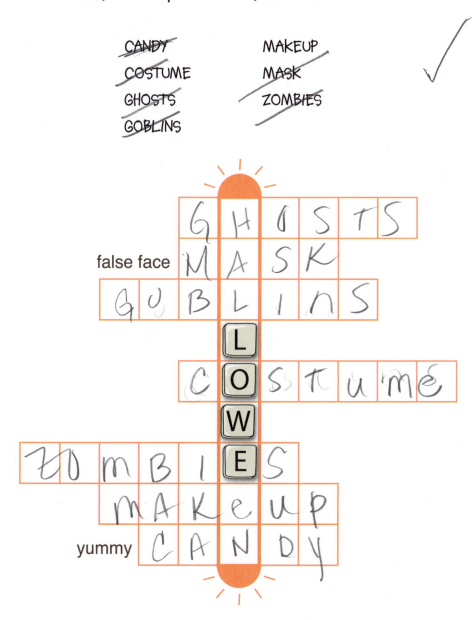

Answer on page 172.

Words All Around! Level

WORD SWATTER

Create eight common words using four letters each from the word below. Letters will be used more than once to form all the words, but only once per word.

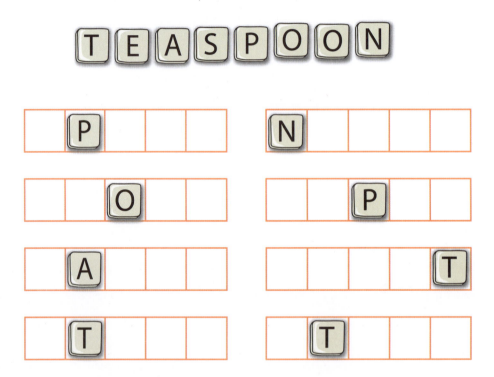

Today, dictionaries contain all sorts of words. But the first English dictionaries, written in the 1600s, were lists of only difficult, new, or uncommon words.

Answer on page 172.

Words All Around!

Level ★ ★

FITTING TILES

In this miniature crossword, the clues are listed randomly. It is up to you to figure out the placement of the nine answers. To help you, we've placed two letters into the grid, and this is the only occurrence of those letters in the completed puzzle.

CLUES

- Japanese animation
- Opposite of first
- Quizzes in school
- Tag on a T-shirt
- Put in chips at the start of a poker game
- Send out
- Spill mark
- Part of a microscope or telescope
- Prejudice

Answer on page 172.

Words All Around! Level

DROP LETTERS

Use all three letter tiles to create four-letter words below. Each tile will be used once per word.

Tiles: I, R, T

S _ _ _

_ _ _ P

D _ _ _

_ _ O _

G _ _ _

_ _ _ M

Level ★ Words All Around!

REPEAT REPEAT

Use the eight tiles given to complete each pair of words. Each pair will use the same four letter tiles in the same order.

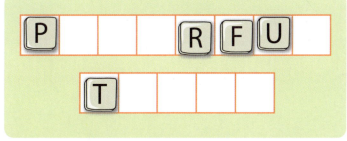

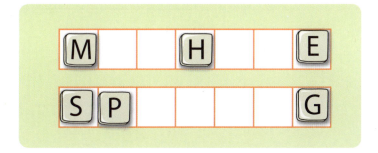

Words All Around! Level

WORD STICKERS

Use the letters given to complete the word pairs.
The words in each pair will be antonyms.

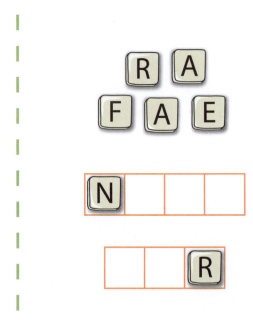

antonym \ˈan-tə-ˌnim\ *noun* : a word of opposite meaning

Answer on page 172.

Level Words All Around!

ONE UP

Use the three tiles at the bottom of the page to solve the bottom clue. Once you do that, move up the page, solving each clue as you go. Carry all the letters used from one clue to the next, rearranging them in the empty spaces.

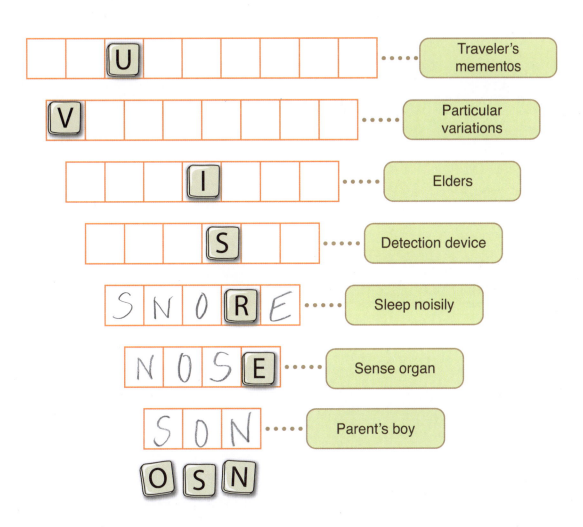

Answer on page 172.

Words All Around! Level

ALPHABET EXPRESS

Use every letter tile below to complete the grid with common words.

Answer on page 173.

Level ★ ★   Words All Around!

LETTER GRIDLOCK

Use the given tiles to complete the grid with words reading across and down. Use the clues, which are in a random order, to help discover the missing words.

CLUES
- Animal that seems to wear a mask
- Ballerinas, for example
- Bedtime tale
- Emergency signal
- Like a desert
- Looks closely
- Makes a big fuss
- Partners of Mas
- Walked back and forth
- Eminem's music

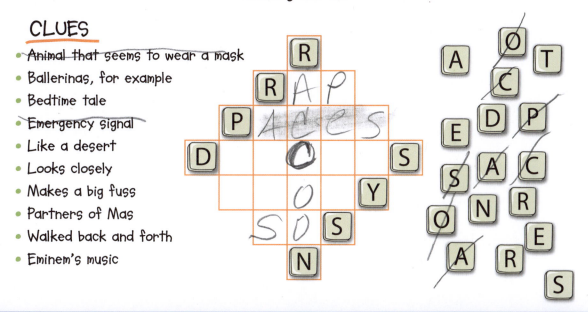

Level ★

JUMBLED UP

Place each letter into the empty boxes below to create a common word. Tiles are in the correct order, but they are not in the upright position.

Words All Around!

Level

WORD SWATTER

Create five common words using three letters each from the two words below. Letters will be used more than once to form all the words, but only once per word.

S A T U P

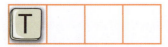

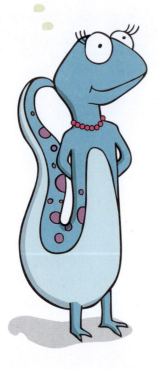

Hmm... what are some words that start with P? Look in the dictionary for a whole list!

Answer on page 173.

Level ★ ★ ★   Words All Around!

SHUFFLE BOARD

Rearrange each of the letters in the words below to form new words. Place the new words into the grid. One letter has already been placed.

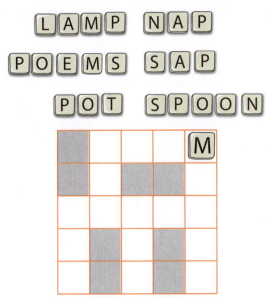

Level ★

REWORD REWIND

Unscramble the tiles to form words that will complete the sentence.

A T R S

The ☐☐☐☐ were neat,

but the talking parrot was the ☐☐☐☐ of the pet parade.

Words All Around!

CRUNCHED LETTERS

Create three words by placing the letter tiles into the grid. Two tiles will be added to each of the three-letter sets given—one letter at the beginning and another at the end.

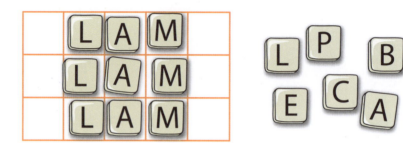

Many English words are borrowed from other languages. Words like "pajamas," "jungle," and "shampoo" all originally came from Hindi, a language spoken in India.

Answer on page 173.

Level ★ Words All Around!

COME TOGETHER

Place each of the tile sets into the empty spaces below to create three nine-letter foods. Each tile set is used only once.

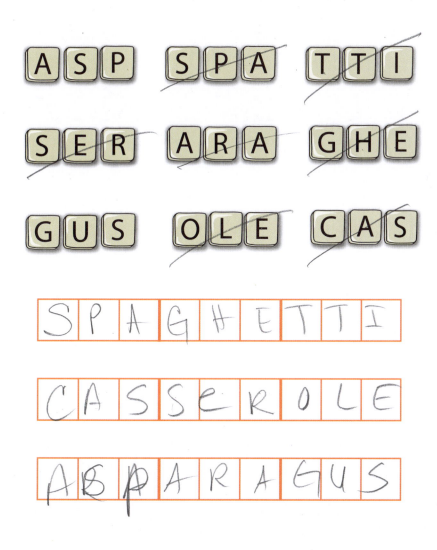

Words All Around! Level

TILE TIE-INS

Using the letter tiles below, complete the grid to reveal the names of 12 animals.

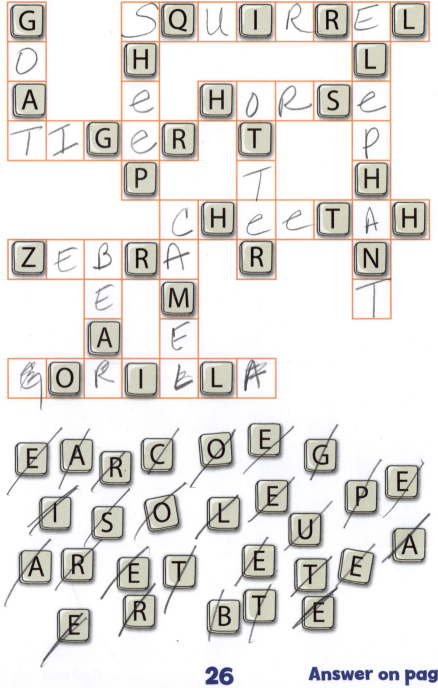

Answer on page 174.

Level ★ ★ Words All Around!

COME TOGETHER

Place each of the tile sets into the empty spaces below to create three nine-letter animals. Each tile set is used only once.

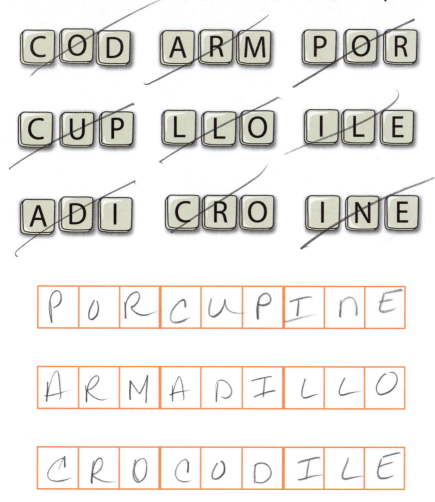

Answer on page 174.

Words All Around! Level ★ ★ ★

FITTING TILES

In this miniature crossword, the clues are listed randomly. It is up to you to figure out the placement of the nine answers. To help you, we've placed two letters into the grid, and this is the only occurrence of those letters in the completed puzzle.

CLUES

- Not on time
- Ruin a secret by telling
- Animal in Peru
- Big fights between countries
- Red root vegetables
- "So, what ____ is new?"
- Underneath
- Leave out
- Up and about

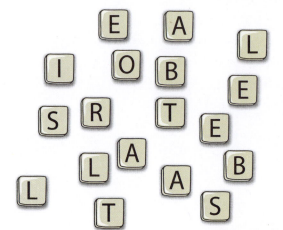
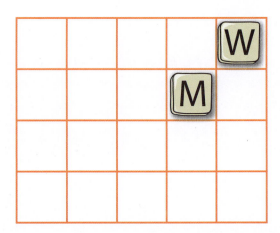

vegetable \\'vej-tə-bəl,\\ *noun* : a plant or plant part (as lettuce, broccoli, or peas) grown for use as food and eaten raw or cooked usually as part of a meal

28   Answer on page 174.

Level ★ ★ Words All Around!

REWORD REWIND

Unscramble the tiles to form words that will complete the sentence.

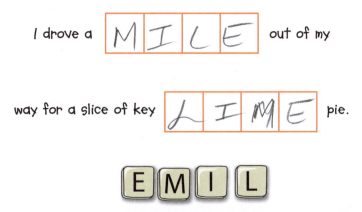

I drove a M I L E out of my way for a slice of key L I M E pie.

E M I L

Level ★

JUMBLED UP

Place each letter into the empty boxes below to create a common word. Tiles are in the correct order, but they are not in the upright position.

Q U I Z

Words All Around! Level

SHUFFLE BOARD

Rearrange each of the letters in the words below to form new words. Place the new words into the grid. One letter has already been placed.

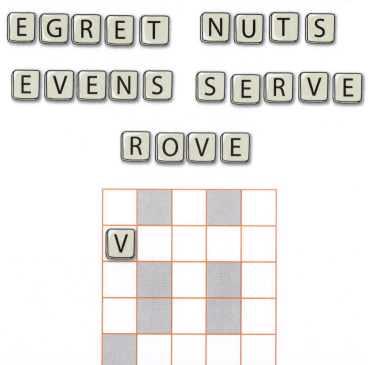

Level

CROSSED OUT

Use the given tiles to spell a pair of words with nearly opposite meanings that meet on the given letter.

Level ★ ★ ★ Words All Around!

DROP LETTERS

Use all three letter tiles to create four-letter words below. Each tile will be used once per word.

Words All Around!

Level ★ ★

ADD-A-LETTER

Rearrange the tiles from each word, adding one new tile from the bottom in order to form the word for a type of facial expression in the empty boxes. Each tile from the bottom of the page is used only once.

grimace \ˈgri-məs\ *noun* : a twisting of the face (as in disgust or pain)

Answer on page 174.

Level ★ ★ ★   Words All Around!

DROP LETTERS

Use all three letter tiles to create four-letter words below.
Each tile will be used once per word.

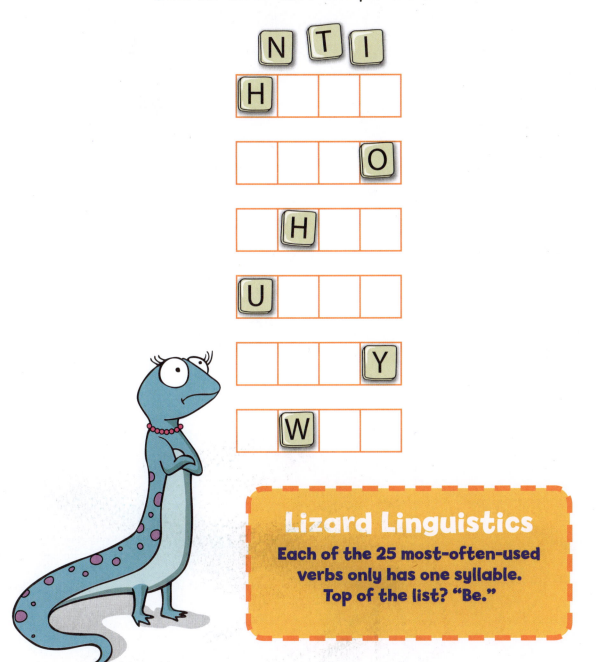

Lizard Linguistics

Each of the 25 most-often-used verbs only has one syllable. Top of the list? "Be."

Answer on page 174.

Words All Around! Level ★ ★ ★

WORD SWATTER

Create ten common words using three letters each from the words below. Letters will be used more than once to form all the words, but only once per word.

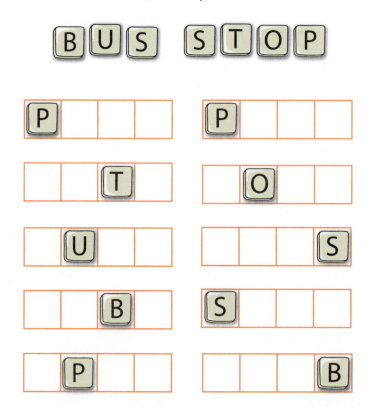

Level  Words All Around!

REWORD REWIND

Unscramble the tiles to form new words that will complete the sentence.

The ☐☐☐ truck driver said my

car would be fixed in ☐☐☐ hours.

Level ★

JUMBLED UP

Place each letter into the empty boxes below to create a common word. Tiles are in the correct order, but they are not in the upright position.

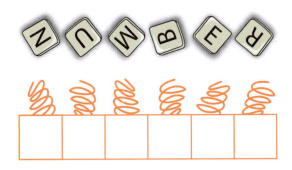

Words All Around! Level

DROP LETTERS

Use all three letter tiles to create four-letter words below. Each tile will be used once per word.

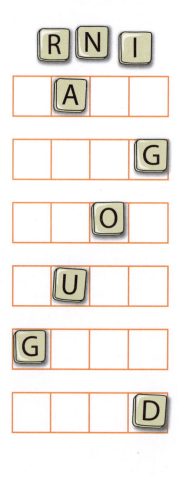

Answer on page 175.

Level ★ ★ ★ Words All Around!

COME TOGETHER

Place each of the tile sets into the empty spaces below to create three nine-letter countries. Each tile set is used only once.

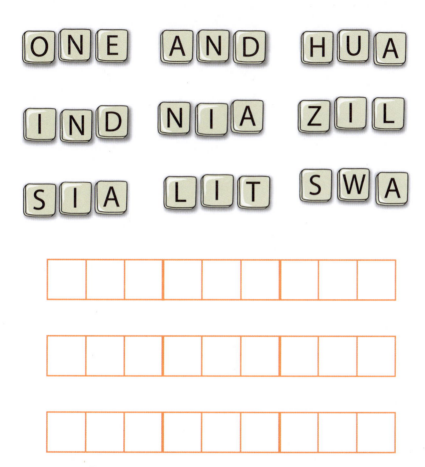

Lizard Linguistics

What word do you use most often to describe something? If you're like most people, the answer is "good," the most commonly used adjective in English.

Words All Around!

Level ★ ★ ★

FITTING TILES

In this miniature crossword, the clues are listed randomly. It is up to you to figure out the placement of the nine answers. To help you, we've placed two letters into the grid, and this is the only occurrence of those letters in the completed puzzle.

CLUES

- Very stubborn animal
- Zodiac sign showing a set of scales
- Not imaginary
- Opposite of minor
- Pokes with a pencil
- Three-legged stand used by artists
- Largest continent
- Giant character in a fairy tale
- The action of putting something to use

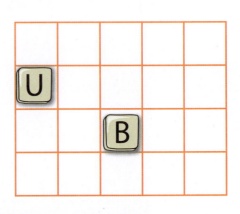

zodiac \zō-dē-ˌak\ *noun* : an imaginary belt in the sky that includes the paths of the planets and is divided into twelve constellations or signs each with a special name and symbol

Answer on page 175.

Level  Words All Around!

WORD STICKERS

Use the letters given to complete the word pairs. The words in each pair will be homophones.

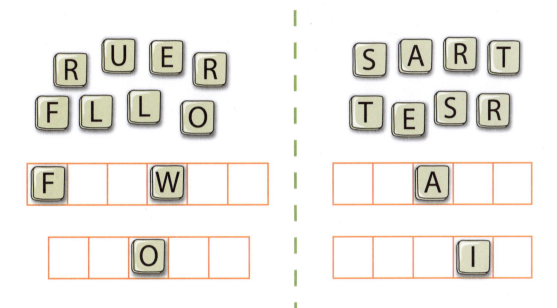

I'm definitely going to need my thinking cap to figure this one out!

homophone \ˈhä-mə-ˌfōn\ *noun* : one of two or more words pronounced alike but different in meaning or origin or spelling

Answer on page 175.

Words All Around! Level

DROP LETTERS

Use all three letter tiles to create four-letter words below. Each tile will be used once per word.

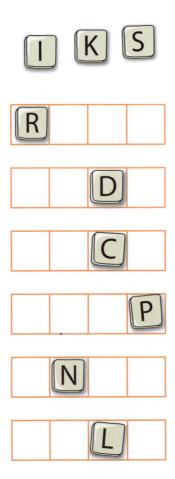

Dictionaries add new words all the time. In the last few years, Merriam-Webster has added words like "binge-watch," "photobomb," and "hangry."

Answer on page 175.

Level ★ Words All Around!

CHAIN WORDS

Place three letters in the middle squares that will complete one word and start another. For example, TAR would complete GUI – TAR – GET.

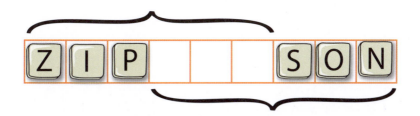

Level ★ ★

REWORD REWIND

Unscramble the tiles to form words that will complete the sentence.

In the haunted warehouse, a ☐☐☐☐☐

might vanish without a ☐☐☐☐☐ .

warehouse \\wer-ˌhau̇s\ *noun* : a building for storing goods and merchandise

Words All Around! Level ★ ★

WORD STICKERS

Use the letters given to complete the word pairs.
The words in each pair will be homophones.

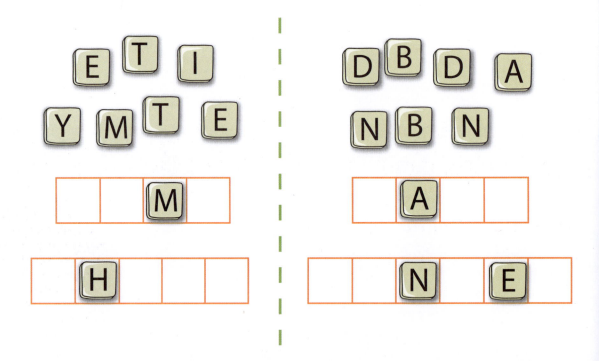

THEME PARK

This "ride" has a theme, but we can't tell you what it is. Place all the words in the boxes below. Then read the word created in the outlined boxes, from top to bottom, to reveal the theme.

BOOTS
COAT
EARMUFFS
GLOVES
HAT
JACKET
LONG UNDERWEAR
MITTENS
SCARF
SWEATER
WOOL SOCKS

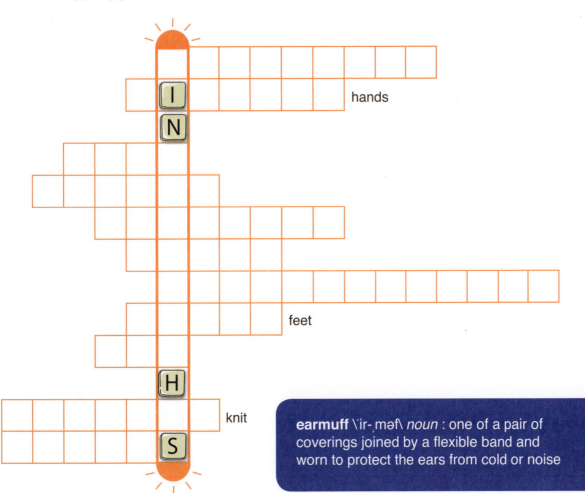

earmuff \ir-məf\ *noun* : one of a pair of coverings joined by a flexible band and worn to protect the ears from cold or noise

Words All Around!

Level

CRUNCHED LETTERS

Create three words by placing the letter tiles into the grid. Two tiles will be added to each of the three-letter sets given—one letter at the beginning and another at the end.

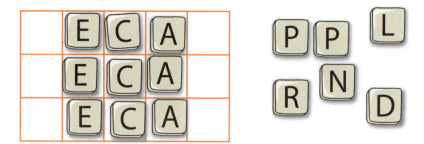

You know what helps me with puzzles? Writing possible answers on a piece of scratch paper.

Answer on page 176.

Level ★ ★ ★ Words All Around!

FITTING TILES

In this miniature crossword, the clues are listed randomly. It is up to you to figure out the placement of the nine answers. To help you, we've placed two letters into the grid, and this is the only occurrence of those letters in the completed puzzle.

CLUES

- Opposite of take
- Bottoms of shoes
- Sound from a horse
- Short afternoon sleeps
- Object that gets worshiped
- _____-visual
- Gardening tools
- Show to be true
- Money in France or Spain

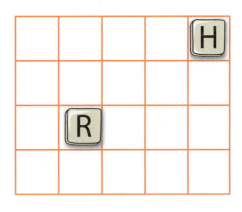

Words All Around! Level

ONE UP

Use the three tiles at the bottom of the page to solve the bottom clue. Once you do that, move up the page, solving each clue as you go. Carry all the letters used from one clue to the next, rearranging them in the empty spaces.

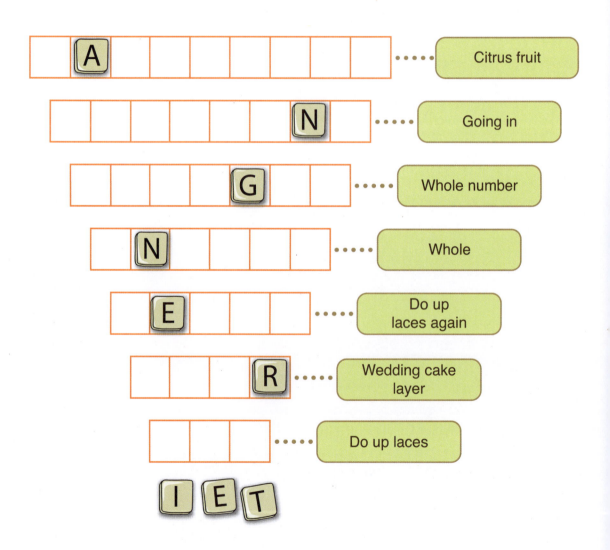

Level ★ ★ ★ Words All Around!

SHUFFLE BOARD

Rearrange each of the letters in the words below to form new words. Place the new words into the grid. One letter has already been placed.

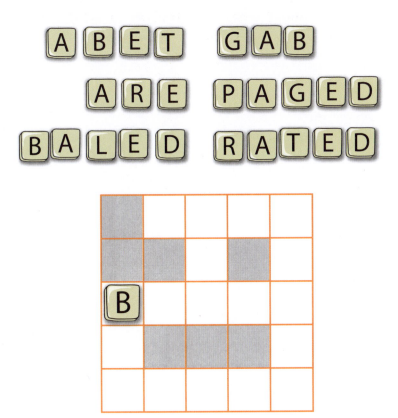

Lizard Linguistics

Who doesn't love to laugh? We've got all sorts of words for laughter, some more obscure than others. Cachinnate, for example, means "to laugh loudly." Guffaw? "A boisterous burst of laughter." And twitter? Not just a website, it's also "a light silly laugh!"

Answer on page 176.

Words All Around! Level

ADD-A-LETTER

Rearrange the tiles from each word, adding one new tile from the bottom in order to form the name of a color in the empty boxes. Each tile from the bottom of the page is used only once.

K I N → ☐ ☐ ☐ ☐

L O G → ☐ ☐ ☐ ☐

G E N E → ☐ ☐ ☐ ☐ ☐

W I T H → ☐ ☐ ☐ ☐ ☐

W O R N → ☐ ☐ ☐ ☐ ☐

R A G → ☐ ☐ ☐ ☐

R E Y P B D

48 Answer on page 176.

LETTER GRIDLOCK

Use the given tiles to complete the grid with words reading across and down. Use the clues, which are in a random order, to help discover the missing words.

CLUES
- Baseball player's hat
- Copy on paper
- Cricket sound
- Dog or goldfish, often
- Freshly painted
- Pitch or pass
- Pixie dust producers
- Took as spouse
- Water faucet
- Writing end of a pencil

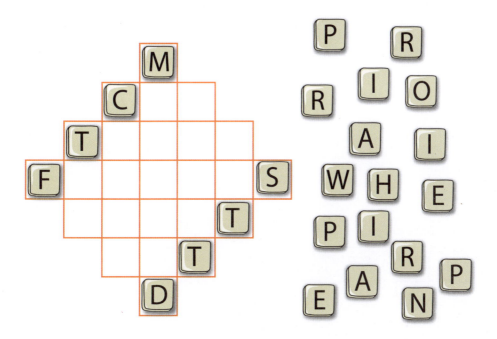

Words All Around! Level

PILES OF TILES

Place all the tiles into the grid so they spell "spacey" words. The tiles are in specific groups. Those groups will appear together in across or down entries.

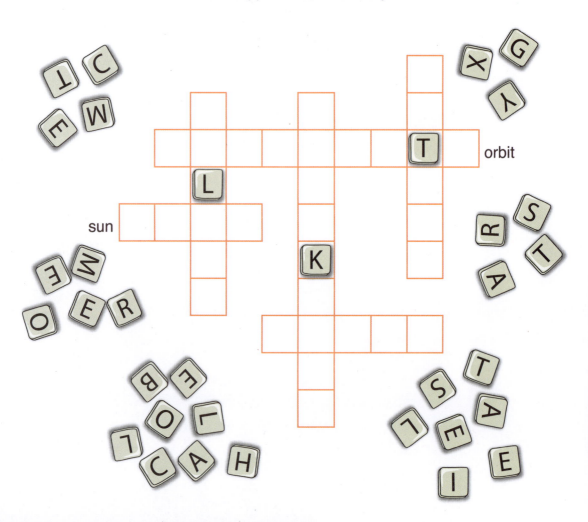

orbit \ȯr-bət\ *noun* : the path taken by one body circling around another body <The earth makes an *orbit* around the sun.>

Answer on page 176.

Level ★ ★ ★ Words All Around!

DROP LETTERS

Use all three letter tiles to create four-letter words below. Each tile will be used once per word.

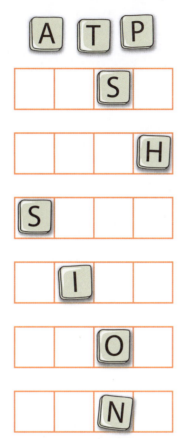

Check it out! No hands!

Words All Around! Level ★ ★ ★

SHUFFLE BOARD

Rearrange each of the letters in the words below to form new words. Place the new words into the grid. One letter has already been placed.

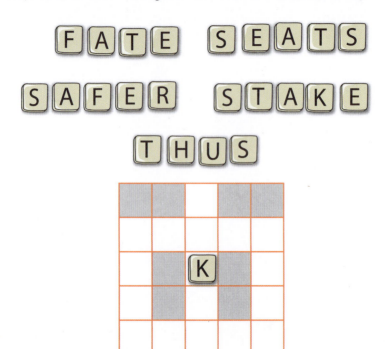

Lizard Linguistics

There are only a few English words with a double-u, like "vacuum," "continuum," "muumuu," and "residuum." Check out "muumuu"—it's got a double double-u!

Answer on page 177.

Level ★ ★ Words All Around!

PLUS ONE

Using the letters in the top three tiles, create three new four-letter words by adding one of the letters from the bottom three tiles.

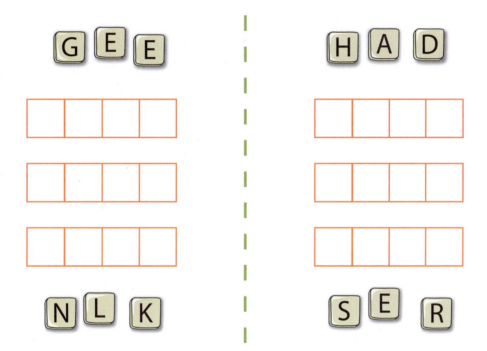

muumuu \ˈmü-ˌmü\ *noun* : a Hawaiian dress that is usually long, loose-fitting, and decorated with bright colors

Words All Around! Level

ADD-A-LETTER

Rearrange the tiles from each word, adding one new tile from the bottom in order to form a vegetable word in the empty boxes. Each tile from the bottom of the page is used only once.

SANE ☐☐☐☐☐

APE ☐☐☐☐

CHAINS ☐☐☐☐☐☐☐

BEST ☐☐☐☐☐

ROC ☐☐☐☐

PRINTS ☐☐☐☐☐☐☐

NOONS ☐☐☐☐☐☐

I N S U P B E

Answer on page 177.

COME TOGETHER

Place each of the tile sets into the empty spaces below to create three nine-letter American cities. Each tile set is used only once.

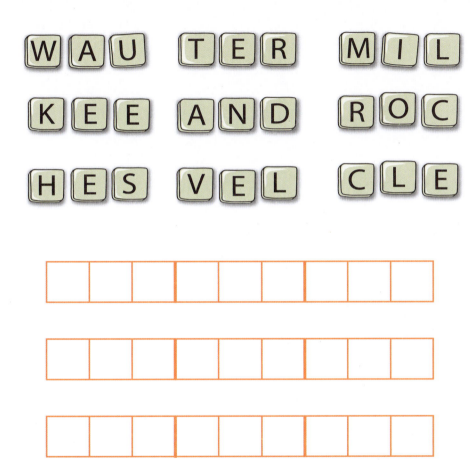

Words All Around!

Words All Around! Level ★ ★ ★

ADD-A-LETTER

Rearrange the tiles from each word, adding one new tile from the bottom in order to form words related to school in the empty boxes. Each tile from the bottom of the page is used only once.

CREATE → ☐☐☐☐☐☐

DUTY → ☐☐☐☐☐

SET → ☐☐☐☐

SEERS → ☐☐☐☐☐☐

PARE → ☐☐☐☐☐

DART → ☐☐☐☐☐

MAX → ☐☐☐☐

C S Y E T H P

education \e-jə-ˈkā-shən\ *noun* : the act or process of teaching or of being taught

Level ★ ★   Words All Around!

WORD SWATTER

Create eight common words using three letters each from the words below. Letters will be used more than once to form all the words, but only once per word.

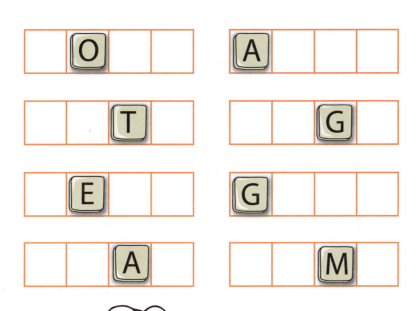

Many English words originally came from Spanish, such as "alligator," "guitar," and "tornado."

Answer on page 177.

Words All Around! Level ★ ★ ★

PILES OF TILES

Place all the tiles into the grid so they spell words related to a twister. The tiles are in specific groups. Those groups will appear together in across or down entries.

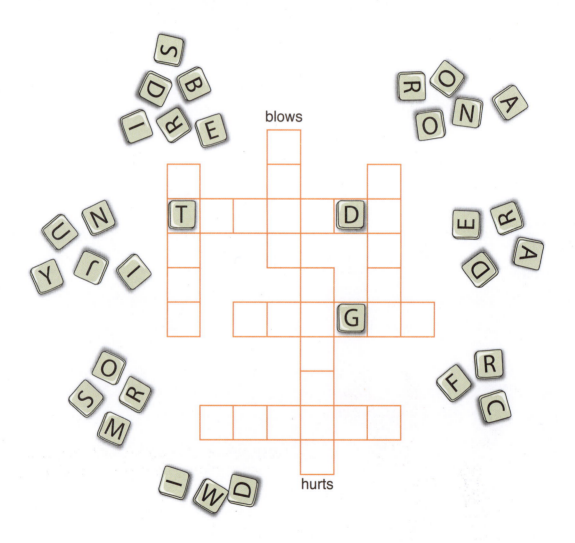

Level ★ ★ Words All Around!

TILE TIE-INS

Using the letter tiles below, complete the grid to reveal the names of ten reptiles and amphibians.

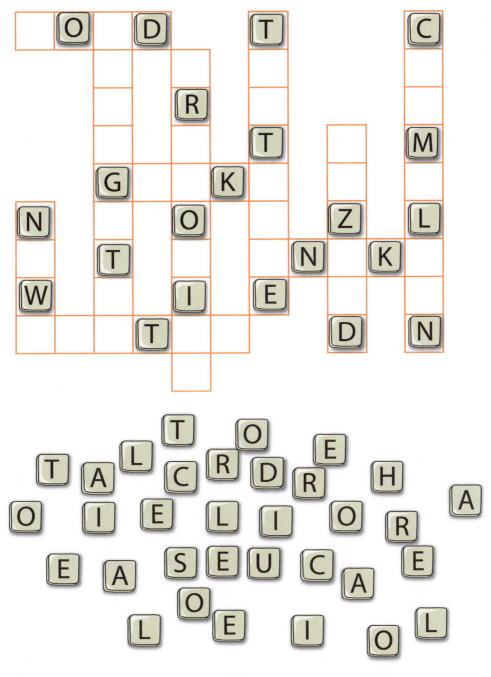

Answer on page 178.

Words All Around! Level

COME TOGETHER

Place each of the tile sets into the empty spaces below to create three nine-letter earth creatures. Each tile set is used only once.

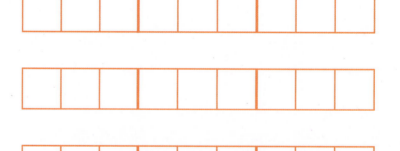

Level ★ ★ Words All Around!

PILES OF TILES

Place all the tiles into the grid so they spell different vegetables. The tiles are compiled in specific groups. Those groups will appear together in across or down entries.

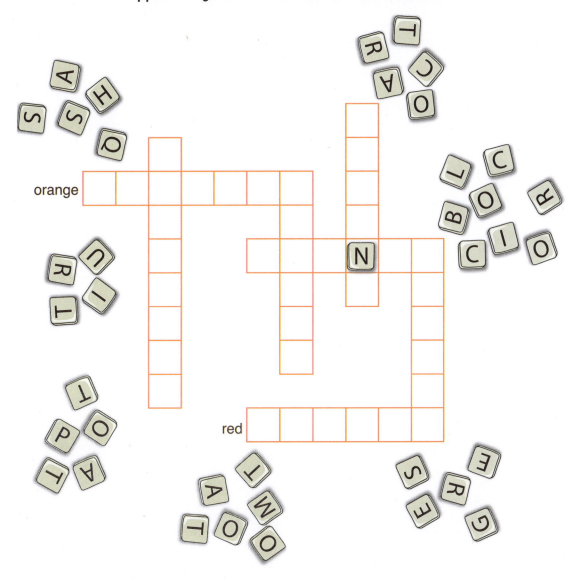

Answer on page 178.

Words All Around! Level ★ ★

DROP LETTERS

Use all three letter tiles to create four-letter words below. Each tile will be used once per word.

[D] [I] [L]

W			

		A	

			E

S			

	E		

		O	

62 Answer on page 178.

Level ★ ★ Words All Around!

PLUS ONE

Using the letters in the top three tiles, create three new four-letter words by adding one of the letters from the bottom three tiles. Do not change the order of the tiles.

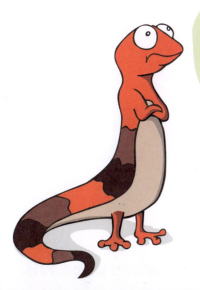

The meaning of a word can change a lot over time. The word "clue" comes from a word that originally meant "a ball of thread or yarn." Any clues to why it changed so much?

Answer on page 178.

Words All Around!

Level ★ ★

THEME PARK

This "ride" has a theme, but we can't tell you what it is. Place all the words in the boxes below. Then read the word created in the outlined boxes, from top to bottom, to reveal the theme.

BED   LATE   SNORE
BLANKET   PAJAMAS   TIRED
GAMES   SNACKS   TV

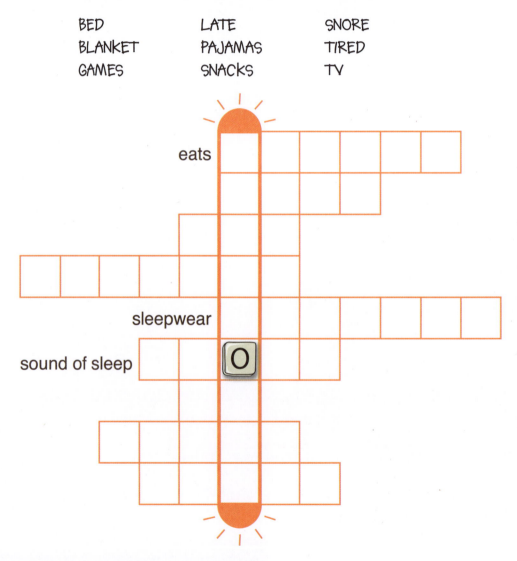

eats

sleepwear

sound of sleep

snack \snak\ *noun* : a small amount of food eaten between meals

Answer on page 178.

Level ★ ★   Words All Around!

REPEAT REPEAT

Use the eight tiles given to complete each pair of words. Each pair will use the same four letter tiles in the same order.

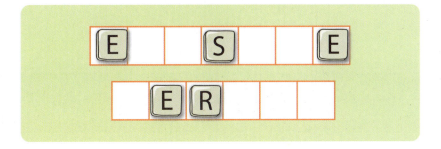

Answer on page 178.

Words All Around! — Level ★ ★

CHAIN WORDS

Place three letters in the middle squares that will complete one word and start another. For example, TAR would complete GUI – TAR – GET.

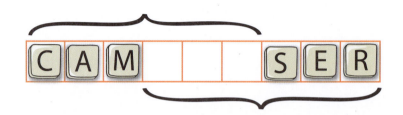

Level ★

REWORD REWIND

Unscramble the tiles to form new words that will complete the sentence.

When cooking chili, my ☐☐☐ decided

to ☐☐☐ more hot sauce.

D D A

Level ★ ★ Words All Around!

PILES OF TILES

Place all the tiles into the grid so they spell different words that have to do with school. The tiles are in specific groups. Those groups will appear together in across or down entries.

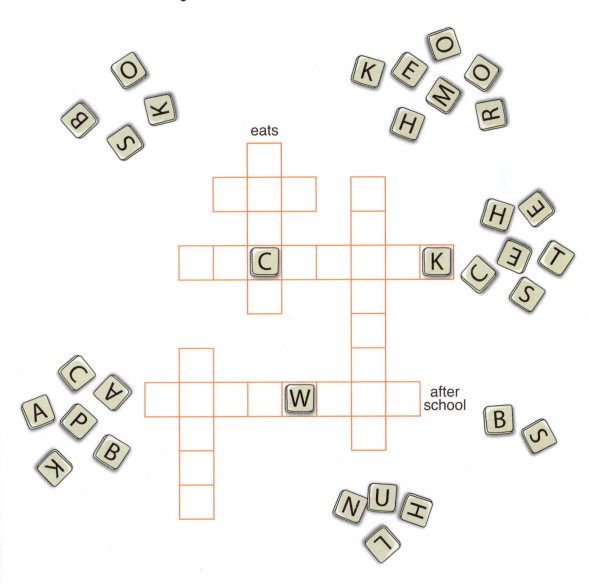

Answer on page 179.

Words All Around! Level

ADD-A-LETTER

Rearrange the tiles from each word, adding one new tile from the bottom in order to form a type of tool in the empty boxes. Each tile from the bottom of the page is used only once.

ELF ☐☐☐☐

LEAP ☐☐☐☐☐

SLICE ☐☐☐☐☐☐

METAL ☐☐☐☐☐☐

HAREM ☐☐☐☐☐☐

PALM ☐☐☐☐☐

NERDS ☐☐☐☐☐☐

M H C A L I N

tool \tül\ *noun* : an instrument used or worked by hand or machine to perform a task

Answer on page 179.

Level ★ ★ ★ Words All Around!

TILE TIE-INS

Using the letter tiles below, complete the grid to reveal the names of 12 states.

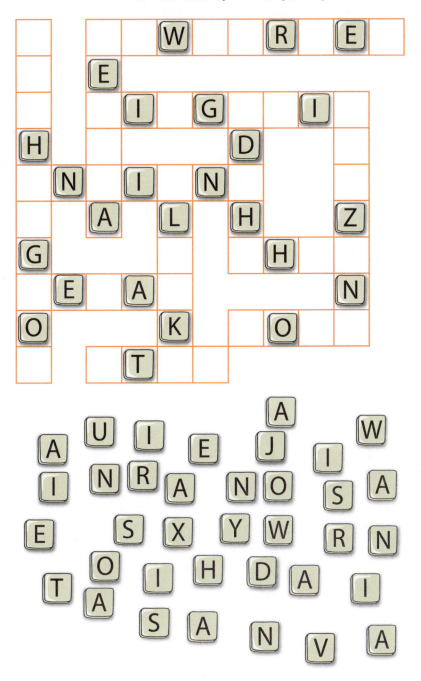

Answer on page 179.

Words All Around! Level

COME TOGETHER

Place each of the tile sets into the empty spaces below to create three nine-letter animals. Each tile set is used only once.

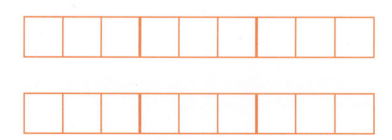

Answer on page 179.

Level   Words All Around!

ADD-A-LETTER

Rearrange the tiles from each word, adding one new tile from the bottom in order to form a vegetable in the empty boxes. Each tile from the bottom of the page is used only once.

S A N E → ☐☐☐☐☐

A P E → ☐☐☐☐

C H A I N S → ☐☐☐☐☐☐

B E S T → ☐☐☐☐☐

R O C → ☐☐☐☐

P R I N T S → ☐☐☐☐☐☐☐

N O O N S → ☐☐☐☐☐☐

I N S U P B E

Answer on page 179.

Words All Around! Level

WORD STICKERS

Use the letters given to complete the word pairs.
Each pair of words will be synonyms of one another.

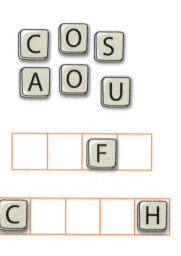

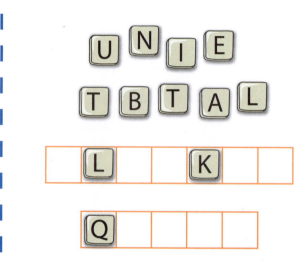

The people who write and edit dictionaries are called "lexicographers."

synonym \si-nə-ˌnim\ *noun* : a word having the same or almost the same meaning as another word in the same language

Answer on page 179.

Level ★ ★ ★   Words All Around!

ADD-A-LETTER

Rearrange the tiles from each word, adding one new tile from the bottom tiles in order to form a type of sport in the empty boxes. Each tile from the bottom of the page is used only once.

LOG → [ ][ ][ ][ ]

LOP → [ ][ ][ ][ ]

STEIN → [ ][ ][ ][ ][ ][ ]

SCORE → [ ][ ][ ][ ][ ][ ]

BURG → [ ][ ][ ][ ][ ]

CHERRY → [ ][ ][ ][ ][ ][ ][ ]

Y N A F C O

Answer on page 179.

Words All Around! Level

TILE TIE-INS

Using the letter tiles below, complete the grid to reveal ten different languages.

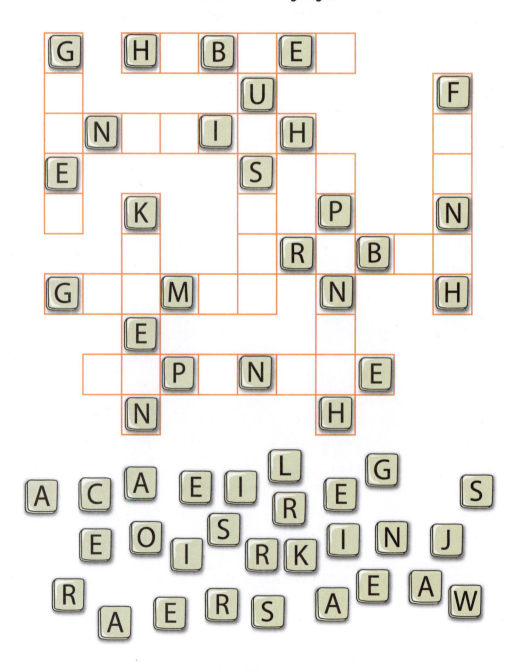

74 Answer on page 180.

Level ★ Words All Around!

LETTER GRIDLOCK

Use the given tiles to complete the grid with words reading across and down. Use the clues, which are in a random order, to help discover the missing words.

CLUES

- Under
- Type of bear
- Prepared for action
- Pig residence
- More elegant
- In favor of
- Listlessness
- Electrical lines
- Drenched
- Boy's name (hidden in "destroyer")

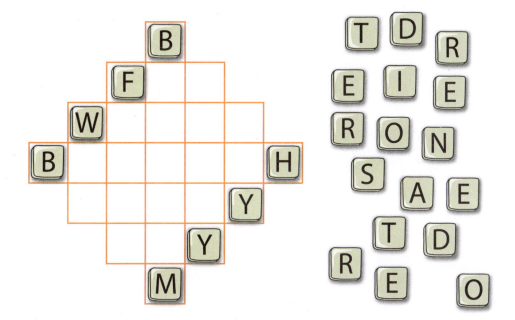

listless \ˈlist-ləs\ *adjective* : too tired or too little interested to want to do things

Answer on page 180.

Words All Around! Level

ONE UP

Use the three tiles at the bottom of the page to solve the bottom clue. Once you do that, move up the page, solving each clue as you go. Carry all the letters used from one clue to the next, rearranging them in the empty spaces.

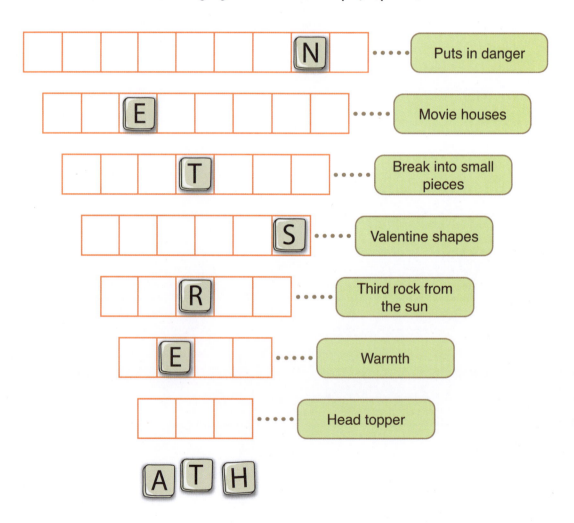

Answer on page 180.

Level ★ ★   Words All Around!

REPEAT REPEAT

Use the eight tiles given to complete each pair of words. Each pair will use the same four letter tiles in the same order.

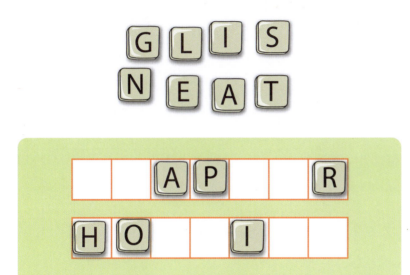

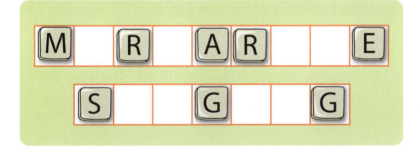

Words All Around! Level

WORD SWATTER

Create six common words using three letters each from the words below. Letters will be used more than once to form all the words, but only once per word.

Level ★

REWORD REWIND

Unscramble the tiles to form words that will complete the sentence.

I went to the store for a  for the

iced tea and a  for the fruit salad.

M E N L O

Answers on page 180.

Level ★ ★ ★   Words All Around!

LETTER GRIDLOCK

Use the given tiles to complete the grid with words reading across and down. Use the clues, which are in a random order, to help discover the missing words.

CLUES

- Go for a target
- Hospital departments
- Accomplished
- Dried with a towel
- Hopelessness
- Mix thoroughly
- Purpose
- Spider's home
- Use them to close your clothes
- Walkway in a theater

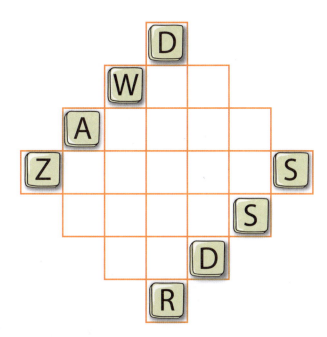

department \di-ˈpärt-mənt\ *noun* : a special part or division of an organization

79   Answer on page 180.

Words All Around!

Level

THEME PARK

This "ride" has a theme, but we can't tell you what it is. Place all the words in the boxes below. Then read the word created in the outlined boxes, from top to bottom, to reveal the theme.

CALL
CASE
EMERGENCY
FRIENDS
HOME

LOL
PARENTS
RINGTONE
TEXTING

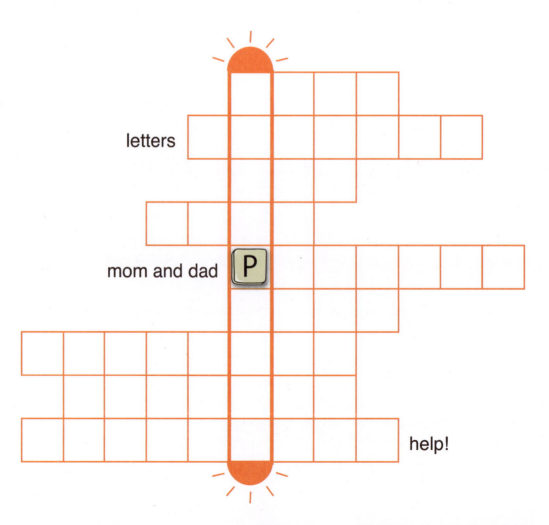

Level ★ ★ ★   Words All Around!

DROP LETTERS

Use all three letter tiles to create four-letter words below. Each tile will be used once per word.

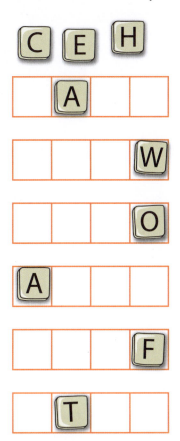

Lizard Linguistics

Contranyms are words that are their own antonyms, such as bolt (meaning both "to secure" and "to run away"), custom ("usual" and "special"), and weather ("withstand" and "wear away"). Can you think of some others?

Answer on page 180.

Words All Around! Level

COME TOGETHER

Place each of the tile sets into the empty spaces below to create three nine-letter creatures. Each tile set is used only once.

Tiles: MEL, BLE, ALL, EON, TOR, BUM, BEE, CHA, IGA

Level ★ ★ **Words All Around!**

THEME PARK

This "ride" has a theme, but we can't tell you what it is. Place all the words in the boxes below. When you do, read the word created in the outlined boxes, from top to bottom, to reveal what the theme is.

ANTS MOSQUITOES
BEETLES ROACHES
FLIES WASPS
GNATS

swarm

E

S

sting

swarm \swȯrm\ *noun* : a large number grouped together and usually in motion

Answer on page 181.

Words All Around! Level

ALPHABET EXPRESS

Use every letter tile below to complete the grid with familiar words.

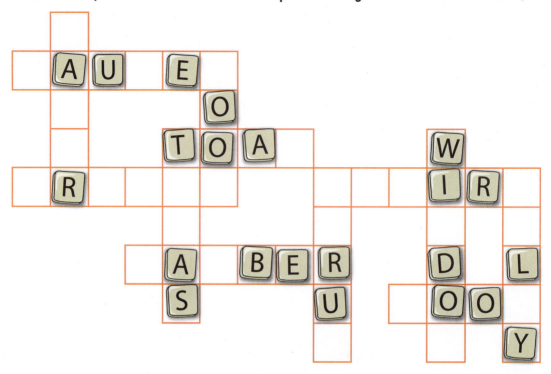

Words All Around!

Level ★

JUMBLED UP

Place each letter into the empty boxes below to create a common word. Tiles are in the correct order, but they are not in the upright position.

Level ★

REWORD REWIND

Unscramble the tiles to form new words that will complete the sentence.

My biggest ☐☐☐☐ is not having

change for bus ☐☐☐☐.

Answers on page 181.

Words All Around! Level

PLUS ONE

Using the letters in the top three tiles, create three new four-letter words by adding one of the letters from the bottom three tiles. Do not change the order of the tiles.

The word "chocolate" originally came from Nahuatl, a language spoken by Native American people in Mexico.

Answer on page 181.

Level ★ ★ ★ Words All Around!

TILE TIE-INS

Using the letter tiles below, complete the grid to reveal eleven weather terms.

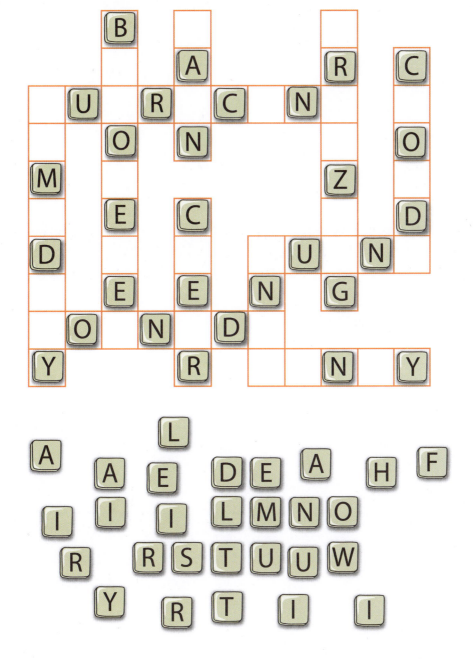

87 Answer on page 181.

Words All Around! Level

SHUFFLE BOARD

Rearrange each of the letters in the words below to form new words. Place the new words into the grid. One letter has already been placed.

LEAP   ROOTS

PLATE   SPOT

RIA   STALE

Level ★ ★

REWORD REWIND

Unscramble the tiles to form words that will complete the sentence.

The truck driver hauling pots and ☐☐☐☐ took some ☐☐☐☐ to get rest before crossing bridges that ☐☐☐☐ the Mississippi River.

A P N S

Answers on page 181.

Words All Around!

Level ★ ★ ★

CRUNCHED LETTERS

Create three words by placing the letter tiles into the grid. Two tiles will be added to the three-letter sets given—one letter at the beginning and another at the end.

Level ★

CHAIN WORDS

Place three letters in the middle squares that will complete one word and start another. For example, TAR would complete GUI – TAR – GET.

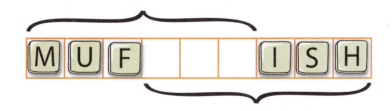

Answers on page 181.

Words All Around! Level

COME TOGETHER

Place each of the tile sets into the empty spaces below to create three nine-letter U.S. states. Each tile set is used only once.

TEN   MEX   SIN

WIS   SEE   NES

NEW   ICO   CON

90   Answer on page 182.

Level   Words All Around!

PILES OF TILES

Place all the tiles into the grid so they spell a rainbow of words. The tiles are in specific groups. Those groups will appear together in across or down entries.

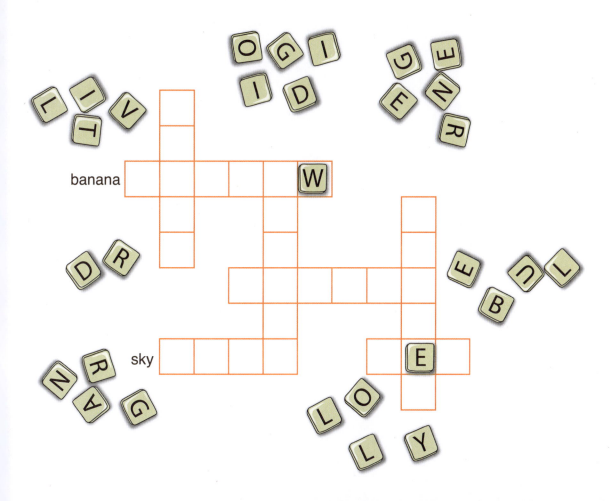

rainbow \ˈrān-ˌbō\ *noun* : an arc of colors that appears in the sky opposite the sun and is caused by the sun shining through mist, rain, or spray

Answer on page 182.

Words All Around! Level

REPEAT REPEAT

Use the eight tiles given to complete each pair of words. Each pair will use the same four letter tiles in the same order.

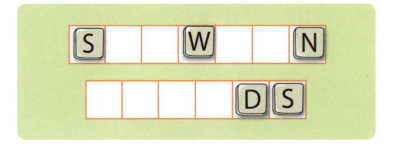

Answer on page 182.

Level ★ ★ ★   Words All Around!

ONE UP

Use the three tiles at the bottom of the page to solve the bottom clue. Once you do that, move up the page, solving each clue as you go. Carry all the letters used from one clue to the next, rearranging them in the empty spaces.

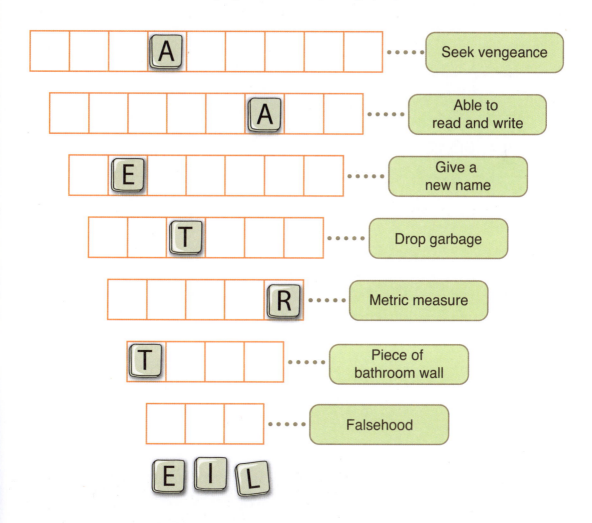

Words All Around!

Level ★ ★ ★

WORD SWATTER

Create ten common words using four letters each from the word below. Letters will be used more than once within the puzzle, but will only be used once per word.

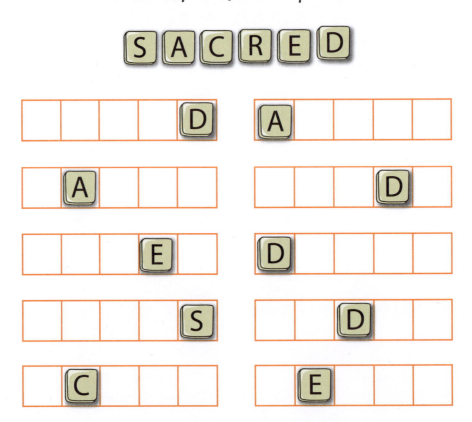

sacred \ˈsā-krəd\ *adjective* **1** : holy **2** : religious **3** : deserving to be respected and honored

Level ★ Words All Around!

DROP LETTERS

Use all three letter tiles to create four-letter words below. Each tile will be used once per word.

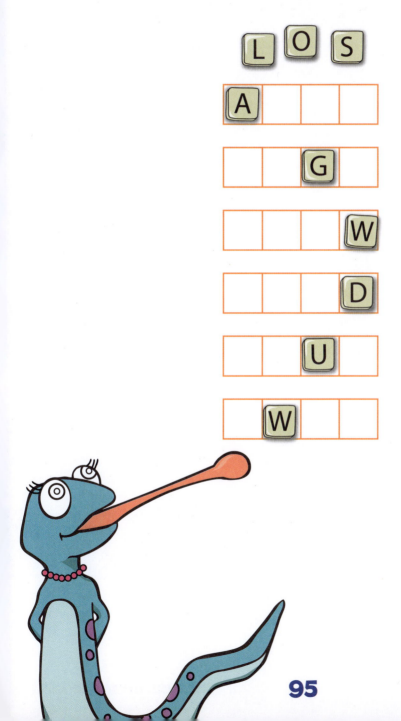

Answer on page 182.

Words All Around!

Level ★

DROP LETTERS

Use all three letter tiles to create four-letter words below. Each tile will be used once per word.

E R U

- C _ _ _
- _ _ L _
- T _ _ _
- _ S _ _
- _ _ D _
- _ _ G _

Answer on page 182.

Level ★ ★ ★ Words All Around!

WORD SWATTER

Create four common words using four letters each from the words below. Letters will be used more than once within the puzzle, but will only be used once per word.

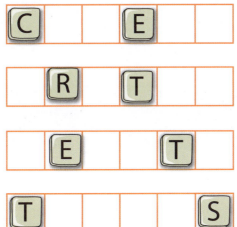

Noah Webster published *An American Dictionary of the English Language* in 1828. He had been working on it for more than 20 years!

Answer on page 182.

Words All Around!

Level ★ ★

CHAIN WORDS

Place three letters in the middle squares that will complete one word and start another. For example, TAR would complete GUI – TAR – GET.

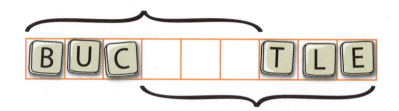

Level ★

JUMBLED UP

Place each letter into the empty boxes below to create a common word. Tiles are in the correct order, but they are not in the upright position.

Words All Around!

Level ★ ★ ★

FITTING TILES

In this miniature crossword, the clues are listed randomly. It is up to you to figure out the placement of the nine answers. To help you, we've inserted two letters in the grid, and this is the only occurrence of those letters in the completed puzzle.

CLUES

- Old cloths used for cleaning
- Makes a noise like a lion
- Region
- Bad guy in a fairy tale
- Circus animals that bark
- Moviemaking places
- Say "hello" to
- Rod and ____ (fishing gear)
- Feel the same way

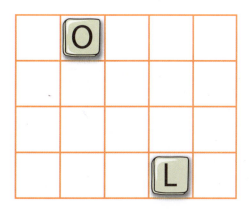

Answer on page 183.

Words All Around!

Level ★ ★

THEME PARK

This "ride" has a theme, but we can't tell you what it is. Place all the words in the boxes below. Then read the word created in the outlined boxes, from top to bottom, to reveal the theme.

AUNT   FATHER   SISTER
BROTHER   MOTHER   UNCLE
COUSIN   NEPHEW

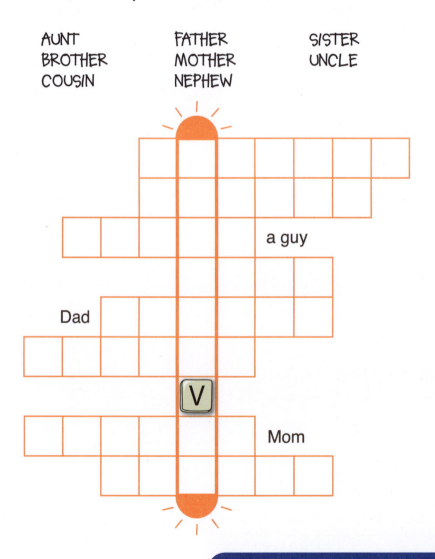

nephew \ne-(,)fyü,\ *noun* : a son of a person's sibling

Answer on page 183.

Level ★ ★   Words All Around!

WORD SWATTER

Create four common words using three letters each from the words below.
Letters will be used more than once within the puzzle,
but will only be used once per word.

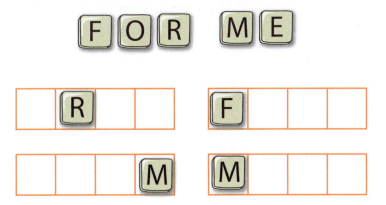

Lizard Linguistics

Estimates range from 250,000 to 1,000,000, but there is no real way to know just how many words are in the English language. What's great about our language is that it's always growing. Merriam-Webster adds hundreds of words and phrases to its dictionaries every year!

Answer on page 183.

Words All Around!

Level

COME TOGETHER

Place each of the tile sets into the empty spaces below to create three nine-letter birds. Each tile set is used only once.

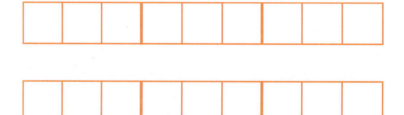

Level ★ ★ Words All Around!

PLUS ONE

Using the letters in the top three tiles, create three new four-letter words by adding one of the letters from the bottom three tiles. Do not change the order of the tiles.

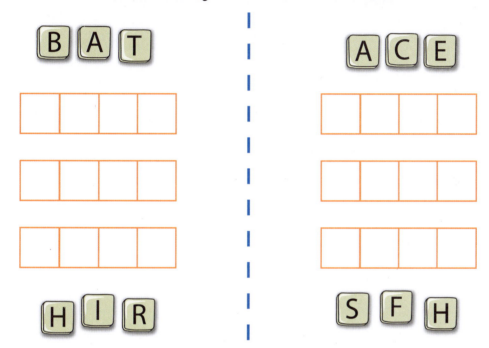

Lizard Linguistics

No single writer has contributed as much to the English language as William Shakespeare. Among the words and phrases that first appeared in his works are: laughable, gloomy, puking, brave new world, lily-livered, and green-eyed monster.

Answer on page 183.

Words All Around!

Level

THEME PARK

This "ride" has a theme, but we can't tell you what it is. Place all the words in the boxes below. Then read the word created in the outlined boxes, from top to bottom, to reveal the theme.

CAMEL LIZARD
DUNES OASIS
HEAT

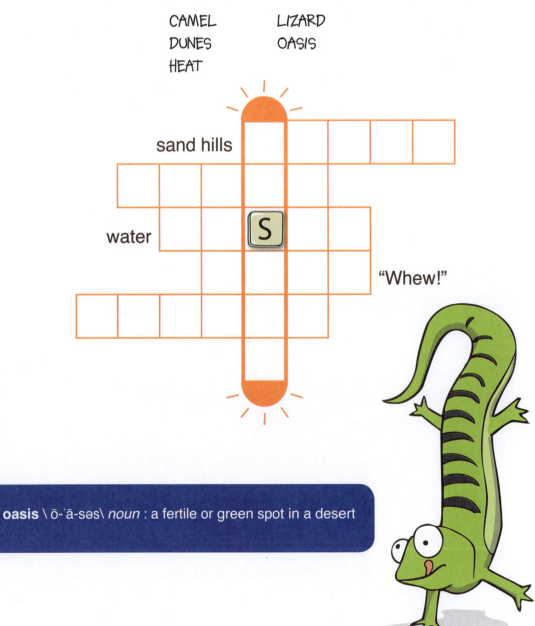

oasis \ ō-'ā-səs\ *noun* : a fertile or green spot in a desert

Answer on page 183.

Level ★ ★ ★   Words All Around!

SHUFFLE BOARD

Rearrange each of the letters in the words below to form new words. Place the new words into the grid. One letter has already been placed.

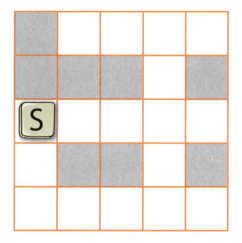

Answer on page 183.

Words All Around! Level

JUMBLED UP

Place each letter into the empty boxes below to create a common word. Tiles are in the correct order, but they are not in the upright position.

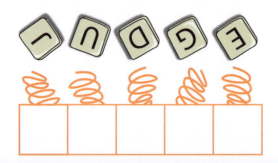

Level ★

SHUFFLE BOARD

Rearrange each of the letters in the tile groups below to form new words. Place the new words into the grid. One letter has already been placed.

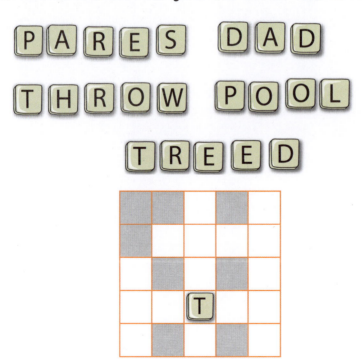

Answers on page 184.

Level ★ ★   **Words All Around!**

REPEAT REPEAT

Use the eight tiles given to complete each pair of words. Each pair will use the same four letter tiles in the same order.

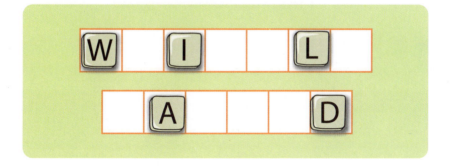

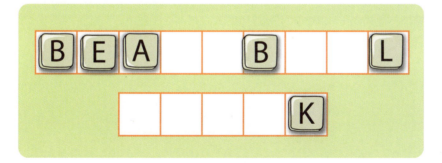

107   Answer on page 184.

Words All Around! Level

CRUNCHED LETTERS

Create three words by placing the letter tiles into the grid. Two tiles will be added to the three-letter sets given—one letter at the beginning and another at the end.

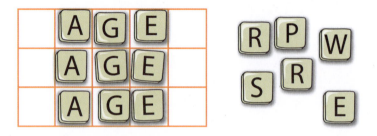

Level ★

JUMBLED UP

Place each letter into the empty boxes below to create a common word. Tiles are in the correct order, but they are not in the upright position.

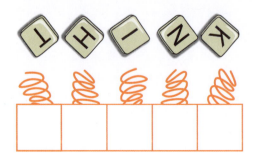

Level ★ ★ Words All Around!

THEME PARK

This "ride" has a theme, but we can't tell you what it is. Place all the words in the boxes below. Then read the word created in the outlined boxes, from top to bottom, to reveal the theme.

CLOCK MIRROR
CLOSET POSTERS
DRESSER TABLE
LAMP

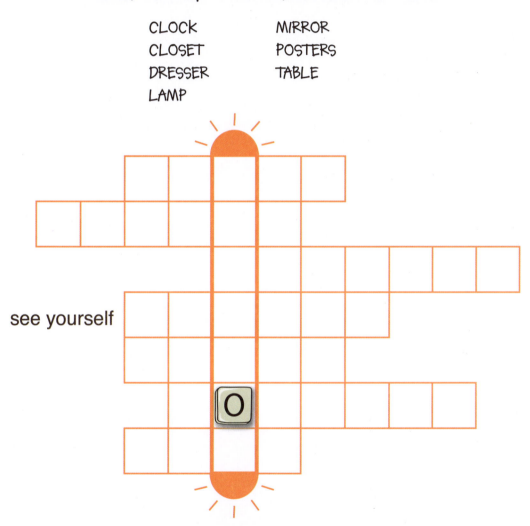

see yourself

dresser \dre-sər\ *noun* : a piece of furniture that has drawers for storing clothing and that sometimes has a mirror

Answer on page 184.

Words All Around! Level

COME TOGETHER

Place each of the tile sets into the empty spaces below to create three nine-letter U.S. states. Each tile set is used only once.

Level

Words All Around!

PILES OF TILES

Place all the tiles into the grid so they spell things you might find at a birthday party. The tiles are in specific groups. Those groups will appear together in across or down entries.

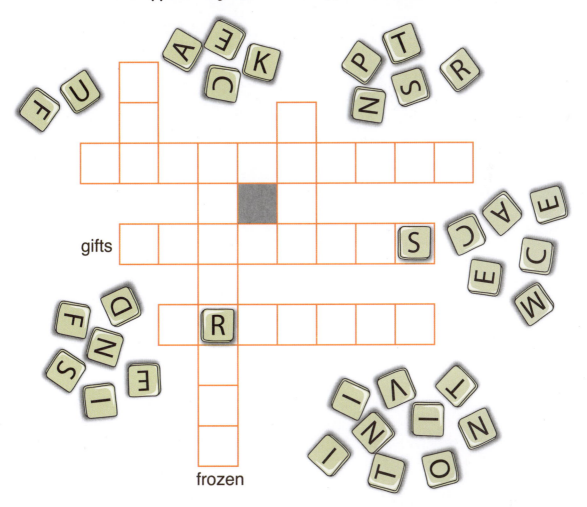

Words All Around!

Level ★ ☆

WORD STICKERS

Use the letters given to complete the word pairs. The words in each pair will be synonyms.

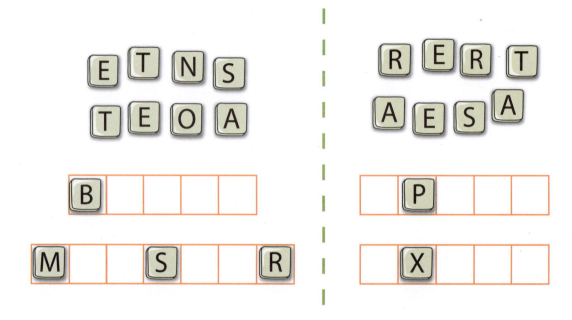

Do you have a favorite letter? I do! Guess what it is!

favorite \ˈfā-vrət\ *adj* : most liked

Level ★ ★ ★   Words All Around!

TILE TIE-INS

Using the letter tiles below, complete the grid to reveal 12 world capitals.

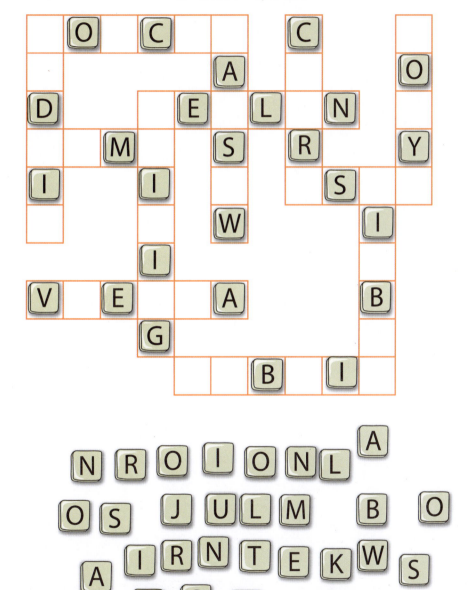

Answer on page 185.

Words All Around!

Level

FITTING TILES

In this miniature crossword, the clues are listed randomly. It is up to you to figure out the placement of the nine answers. To help you, we've placed two letters in the grid, and this is the only occurrence of those letters in the completed puzzle.

CLUES

- People older than 12 but younger than 20
- "Keep quiet!"
- Abandon
- Wedding cake layer
- Our planet
- July 4, 1776, is an example of one
- "Goodbye," in French
- Penny coin
- Bright thought

Languages have families, just like people! English is in the Germanic language family and is closely related to German and Dutch.

abandon \ə-ˈban-dən\ *verb* : to leave and never return : give up completely

Answer on page 185.

Level ★ ★   Words All Around!

CRUNCHED LETTERS

Create three words by placing the letter tiles into the grid. Two tiles will be added to the three-letter sets given—one letter at the beginning and another at the end.

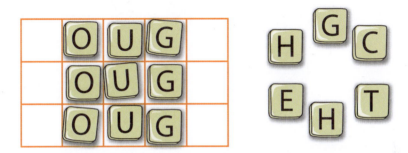

Level ★

JUMBLED UP

Place each letter into the empty boxes below to create a common word. Tiles are in the correct order, but they are not in the upright position.

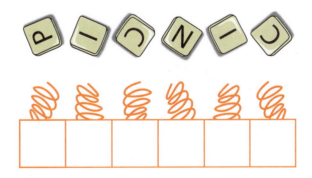

Words All Around!

Level ★ ★ ★

DROP LETTERS

Use all three letter tiles to create four-letter words below. Each tile will be used once per word.

Tiles: W D E

	I		

O			

		L	

	R		

A			

			Y

Level ★   Words All Around!

PLUS ONE

Using the letters in the top three tiles, create three new four-letter words by adding one of the letters from the bottom three tiles. Do not change the order of the tiles.

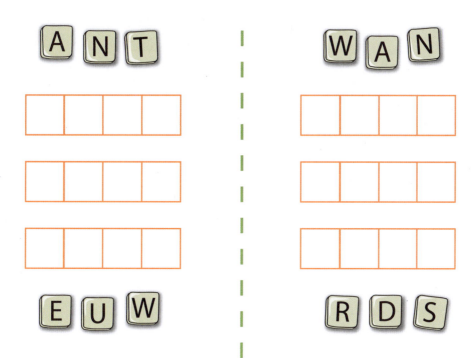

Lizard Linguistics

There are 26 letters in the English alphabet, and some sentences—called "pangrams"—use them all! Probably the most famous example is "The quick brown fox jumps over the lazy dog." Others are a little spookier, like "Sphinx of black quartz, judge my vow" (which is only 29 total letters!).

Answer on page 185.

Words All Around! Level

PILES OF TILES

Place all the tiles into the grid so they spell major U.S. cities. The tiles are in specific groups. Those groups will appear together in across or down entries.

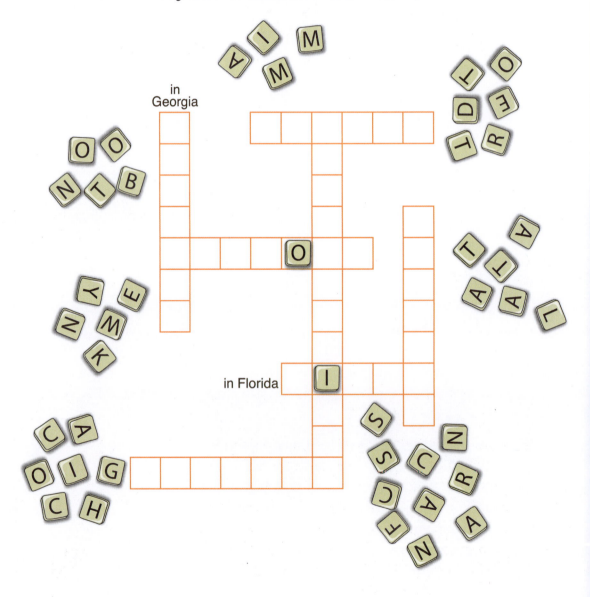

Level ★ ★ ★ Words All Around!

CHAIN WORDS

Place three letters in the middle squares that will complete one word and start another. For example, TAR would complete GUI – TAR – GET.

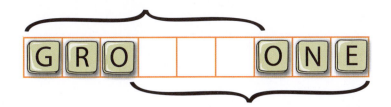

Level ★

JUMBLED UP

Place each letter into the empty boxes below to create a common word. Tiles are in the correct order, but they are not in the upright position.

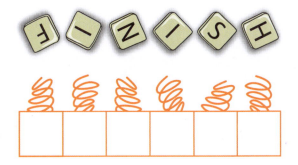

Answers on page 185.

Words All Around! Level

DROP LETTERS

Use all three letter tiles to create four-letter words below. Each tile will be used once per word.

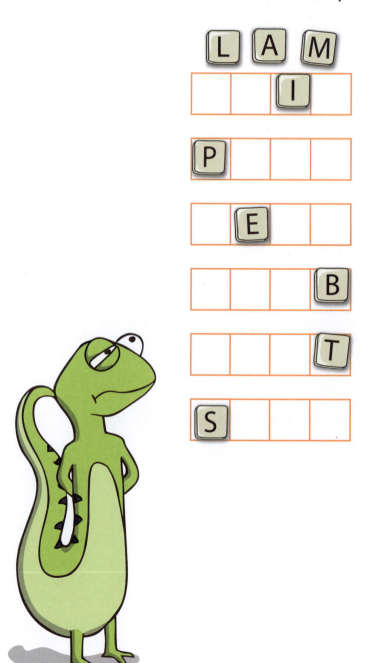

Answer on page 185.

Level ★ ★ ★ Words All Around!

WORD SWATTER

Create three common words using four letters each from the words below. Letters will be used more than once within the puzzle, but will only be used once per word.

> Noah Webster's dictionary was the first to be written in America. He included many American words, like "skunk" and "chowder," that were not listed in British dictionaries.

chowder \chau̇-dər\ *noun* : a soup or stew made of fish, clams, or a vegetable usually simmered in milk

Answer on page 185.

Words All Around! Level ★ ★ ★

ONE UP

Use the three tiles at the bottom of the page to solve the bottom clue. Once you do that, move up the page, solving each clue as you go. Carry all the letters used from one clue to the next, rearranging them in the empty spaces.

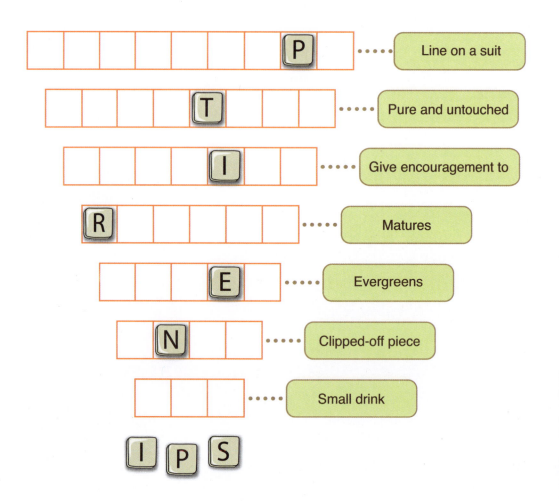

Level ★ Words All Around!

CHAIN WORDS

Place two letters in the middle squares that will complete one word and start another. For example, ER would complete FLI – ER – ROR.

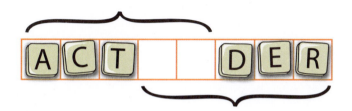

Level ★

CROSSED OUT

Use the given tiles to spell a pair of words with opposite meanings that meet on the given letter.

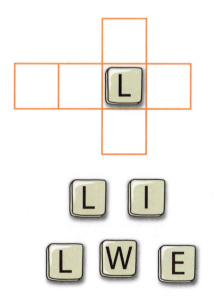

Answers on page 186.

Words All Around!

Level ★

JUMBLED UP

Place each letter into the empty boxes below to create a common word. Tiles are in the correct order, but they are not in the upright position.

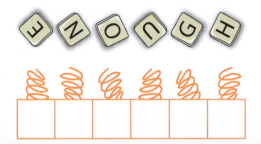

Level ★

ADD-A-LETTER

Rearrange the tiles from each word, adding one new tile from the bottom in order to spell parts of the leg in the empty boxes. Each tile from the bottom of the page is used only once.

TOO

LEE

HIS

LANE

EKE

N N K H F

Answers on page 186.

Level Words All Around!

REPEAT REPEAT

Use the eight tiles given to complete each pair of words. Each pair will use the same four letter tiles in the same order.

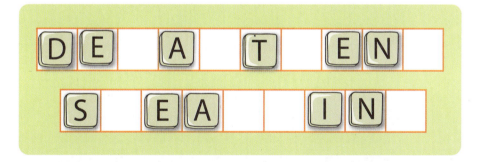

125   Answer on page 186.

Words All Around! Level

CRUNCHED LETTERS

Create three words by placing the letter tiles into the grid. Two tiles will be added to the three-letter sets given— one letter at the beginning and another at the end.

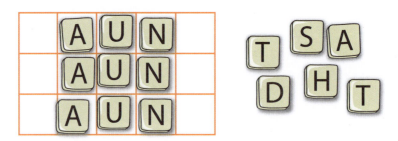

Lizard Linguistics

A palindrome is a word or phrase that can be read the same either forward or backward. "Mom" is one example; "deed" is another. Some palindromes run much, much longer than that. In fact, French writer Georges Perec created a palindrome that was 5,556 letters long!

Level ★ ★ ★   Words All Around!

TILE TIE-INS

Using the letter tiles below, complete the grid to reveal ten elements from the periodic table.

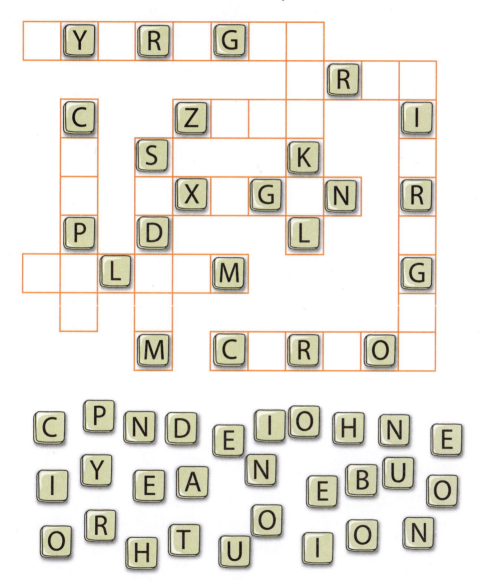

Answer on page 186.

Words All Around! Level

PLUS ONE

Using the letters in the top three tiles, create three new four-letter words by adding one of the letters from the bottom three tiles. Do not change the order of the tiles.

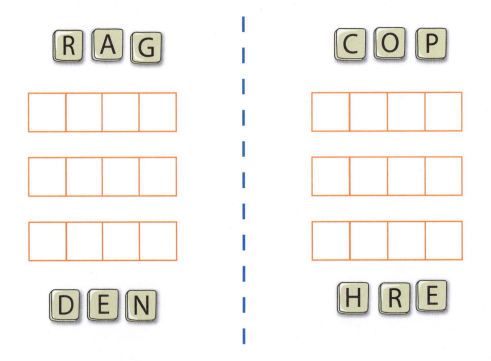

puzzle \pə-zəl\ *noun* 1 : a question, problem, or device intended to test skill or cleverness 2 : something that perplexes

Level ★ ★ — Words All Around!

COME TOGETHER

Place each of the tile sets into the empty spaces below to create three nine-letter American cities. Each tile set is used only once.

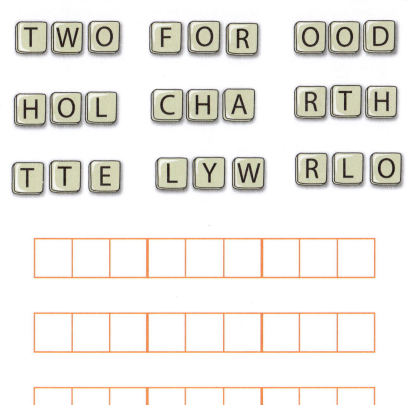

Words All Around!

FITTING TILES

In this miniature crossword, the clues are listed randomly. It is up to you to figure out the placement of the nine answers. To help you, we've placed two letters in the grid, and this is the only occurrence of those letters in the completed puzzle.

CLUES

- Type of fish
- Spending splurge
- AM/FM item in a car's dashboard
- Circle pieces
- Future oak tree
- Smell
- Part of your face used for smelling
- Christian symbol
- Get out of bed

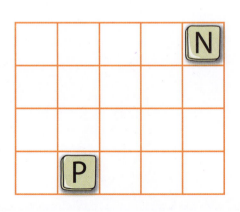

splurge \splərj\ *verb* : to spend lavishly or give in to indulgence

Answer on page 187.

Level ★ ★ Words All Around!

WORD SWATTER

Create four words using three letters each from the words below. Letters will be used more than once within the puzzle, but will only be used once per word.

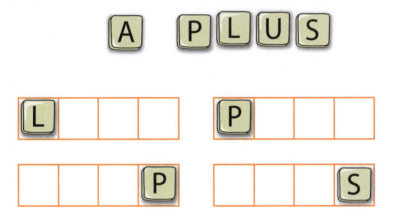

Words All Around! Level

ALPHABET EXPRESS

Use every letter tile below to complete the grid with common words.

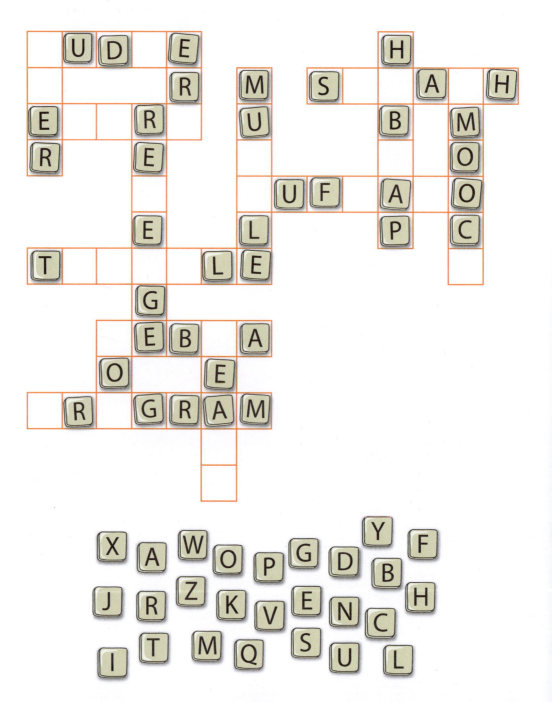

Answer on page 187.

Level ★ ★ Words All Around!

SHUFFLE BOARD

Rearrange the letters in each of the words below to form new words. Place the new words into the grid. One letter has already been placed.

Answer on page 187.

Words All Around! Level

REPEAT REPEAT

Use the eight tiles given to complete each pair of words. Each pair will use the same four letter tiles in the same order.

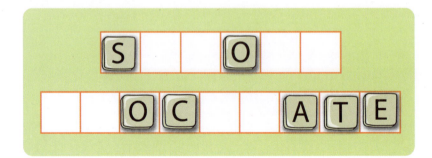

Level ★ ★ **Words All Around!**

COME TOGETHER

Place each of the tile sets into the empty spaces below to create three nine-letter countries. Each tile set is used only once.

INA TAR LIA

AUS COS ENT

ARG ICA TRA

135 Answer on page 187.

Words All Around! — Level

PILES OF TILES

Place all the tiles into the grid so they spell terms related to the word "bicycle." The tiles are in specific groups. Those groups will appear together in across or down entries.

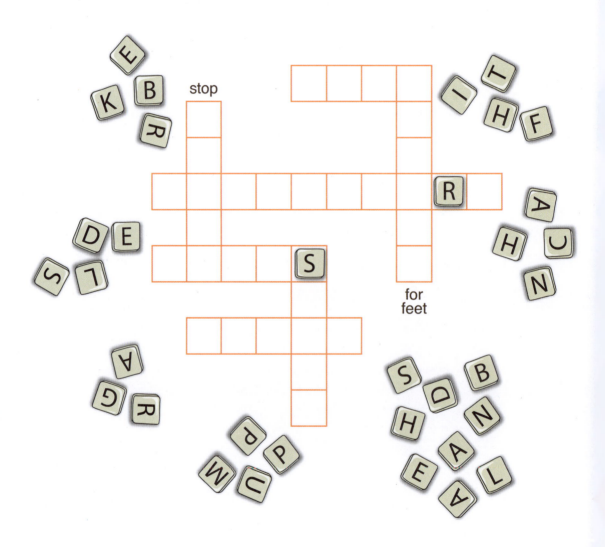

136 Answer on page 187.

Level ★ Words All Around!

CHAIN WORDS

Place two letters in the middle squares that will complete one word and start another. For example, ER would complete FLI – ER – ROR.

Answer on page 187.

Level ★ ★

ADD-A-LETTER

Rearrange the tiles from each word, adding one new tile from the bottom in order to form words that refer to family members in the empty boxes. Each tile from the bottom of the page is used only once.

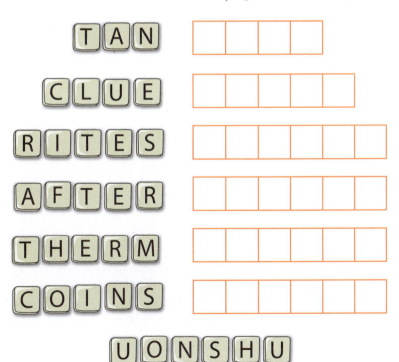

Answer on page 188.

Words All Around!

THEME PARK

This "ride" has a theme, but we can't tell you what it is. Place all the words in the boxes below. Then read the word created in the outlined boxes, from top to bottom, to reveal the theme.

- BIKE
- CAR
- GEAR
- SKATES
- STORAGE
- YARD TOOLS

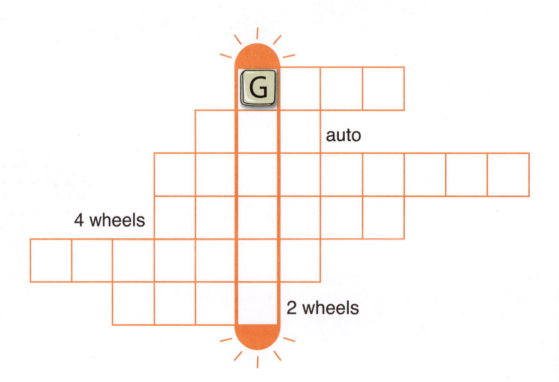

storage \stȯr-ij\ *noun* : space or a place for putting things for future use or for safekeeping

Level   Words All Around!

WORD SWATTER

Create eight common words using three letters each from the word below. Letters will be used more than once within the puzzle, but will only be used once per word.

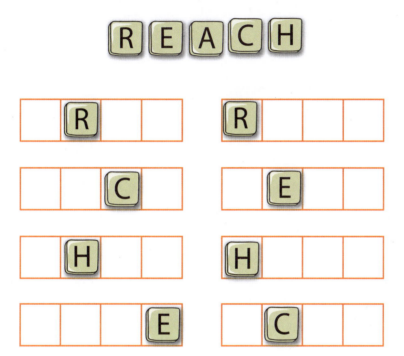

139   Answer on page 188.

Words All Around! Level

WORD SWATTER

Create six common words using five letters each from the word below. Letters will be used more than once within the puzzle, but will only be used once per word.

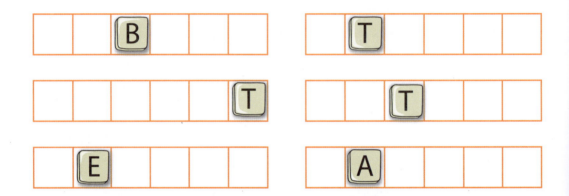

Lizard Linguistics

Ever switch the letters around in a sentence? Then you've stumbled into a "spoonerism!" Named after Reverend William Archibald Spooner, spoonerisms are when you unintentionally swap sounds to wake new mords. Er...that's make new words!

Answer on page 188.

Level ★ ★ Words All Around!

ALPHABET EXPRESS
Use every letter tile below to complete the grid with familiar words.

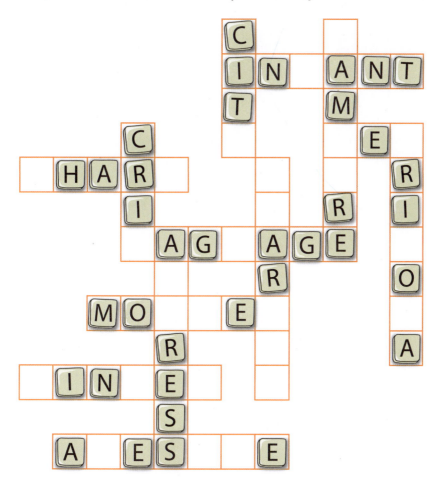

Answer on page 188.

Words All Around! Level

TILE TIE-INS

Using the letter tiles below, complete the grid to reveal nine types of ice cream toppings.

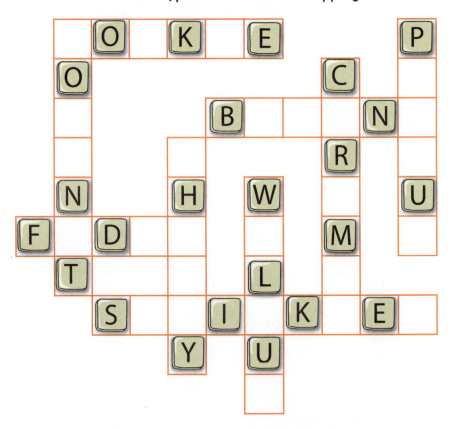

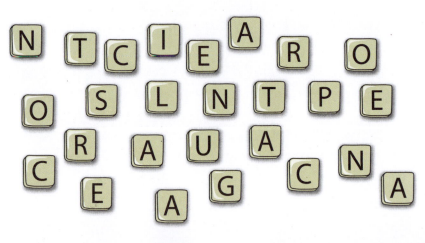

142 Answer on page 188.

Level ★ ★ ★   Words All Around!

CRUNCHED LETTERS

Create three words by placing the letter tiles into the grid. Two tiles will be added to the three-letter sets given—one letter at the beginning and another at the end.

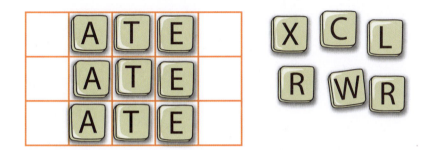

Level ★

JUMBLED UP

Place each letter into the empty boxes below to create a common word. Tiles are in the correct order, but they are not in the upright position.

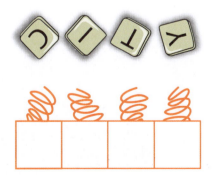

Answers on page 188.

Words All Around! Level

ADD-A-LETTER

Rearrange the tiles from each word, adding one new tile from the bottom in order to form a type of cheese in the empty boxes. Each tile from the bottom of the page is used only once.

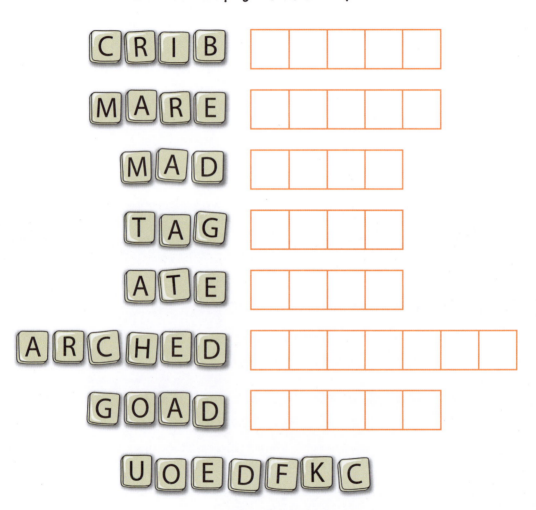

cheese \chēz\ *noun* : the curd of milk pressed for use as food

Level ★ Words All Around!

REPEAT REPEAT

Use the eight tiles given to complete each pair of words. Each pair will use the same four letter tiles in the same order.

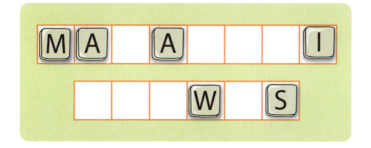

Words All Around!

Level ★

WORD STICKERS

Use the letters given to complete the word pairs. The words in each pair will be homophones.

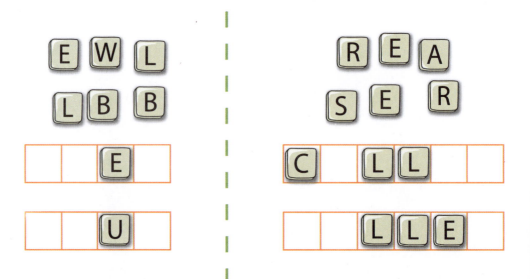

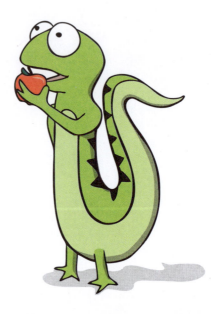

Here's a hint: One of the answers is very colorful.

Answer on page 189.

Level ★ ★ ★   Words All Around!

LETTER GRIDLOCK

Use the given tiles to complete the grid with words reading across and down. Use the clues, which are in a random order, to help discover the missing words.

CLUES

- "___ Goes the Weasel"
- A note to follow fa
- Drinking tube
- Fuel for a car
- Like a house full of ghosts
- Part of a bloom
- Pull thread with a needle
- Sticks out the bottom lip
- Tight braid of hair
- Wounds with a tusk

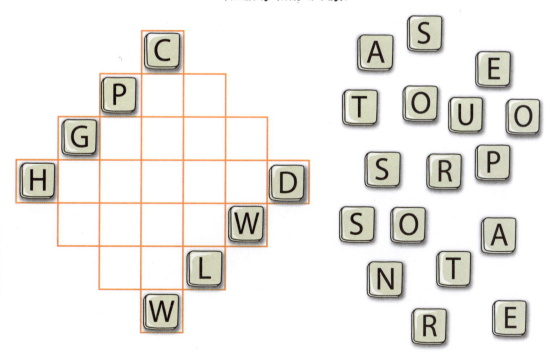

Answer on page 189.

Words All Around! Level ★ ★ ★

COME TOGETHER

Place each of the tile sets into the empty spaces below to create three nine-letter birds. Each tile set is used only once.

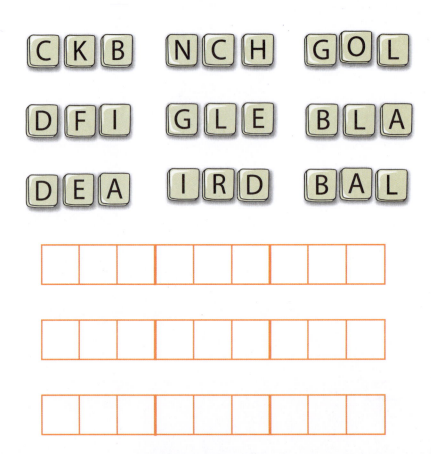

aviary \ˈā-vē-ˌer-ē\ *noun* : a place (as a large cage or a building) where birds are kept

Answer on page 189.

Level   Words All Around!

JUMBLED UP

Place each letter into the empty boxes below to create a common word. Tiles are in the correct order, but they are not in the upright position.

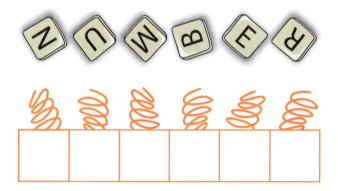

Lizard Linguistics

Did you know that sandwiches are named after a person: the fourth Earl of Sandwich? That makes sandwich an "eponym": a word that comes from a name, whether it's the name of a person, place, or character. Other eponyms include "mesmerize," "boycott," "jumbo," and "mentor."

Words All Around!

Level ★ ★

REPEAT REPEAT

Use the eight tiles given to complete each pair of words.
Each pair will use the same four letter tiles in the same order.

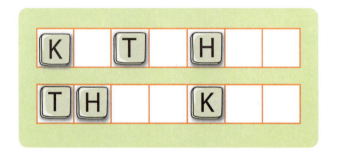

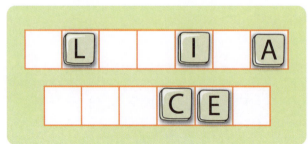

Level  Words All Around!

ONE UP

Use the three tiles at the bottom of the page to solve the bottom clue. Once you do that, move up the page, solving each clue as you go. Carry all the letters used from one clue to the next, rearranging them in the empty spaces.

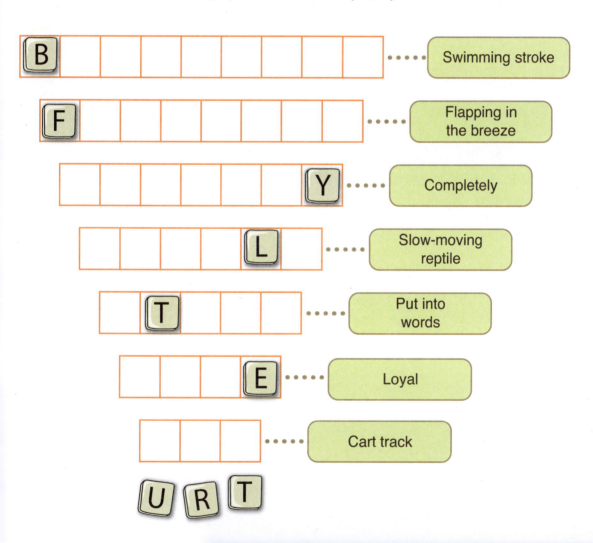

reptile \'rep-ˌtī(-ə)l\ *noun* : a cold-blooded animal (as a snake, lizard, or alligator) that breathes air and usually has the skin covered with scales or bony plates

Answer on page 189.

Words All Around!

CHAIN WORDS

Place two letters in the middle squares that will complete one word and start another. For example, ER would complete FLI – ER – ROR.

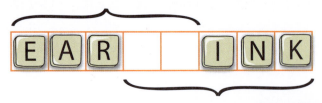

Answer on page 189.

Level ★ ★

CROSSED OUT

Use the given tiles to spell a pair of related words that meet on the given letter.

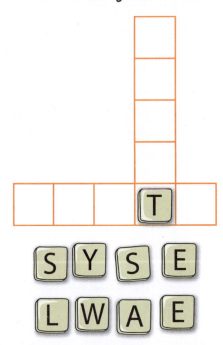

Answer on page 190.

Level ★ ★ Words All Around!

PLUS ONE

Using the letters in the top three tiles, create three new four-letter words by adding one of the letters from the bottom three tiles. Do not change the order of the tiles.

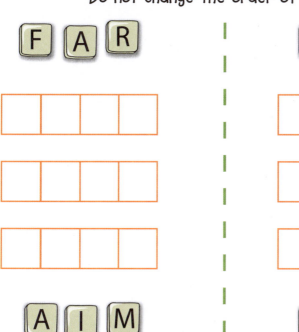

English has borrowed words from lots of different languages. Arabic has given us words like "magazine," "lemon," and "sofa."

Answer on page 190.

Words All Around!

Level ★

ADD-A-LETTER

Rearrange the tiles from each word, adding one new tile from the bottom in order to form a type of transportation in the empty boxes. Each tile from the bottom of the page is used only once.

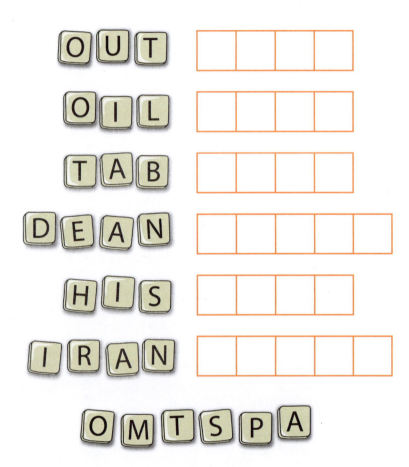

transportation \tran(t)s-pər-'tā-shən\ *noun* : an act, instance, or means of carrying people or goods from one place to another or of being carried from one place to another

Answer on page 190.

Level ★ ★ ★ **Words All Around!**

COME TOGETHER

Place each of the tile sets into the empty spaces below to create three nine-letter birds. Each tile set is used only once.

Tiles: D P I | D G E | B L A | P E R | C K T | S A N | T R I | E R N | P A R

Words All Around!

ALPHABET EXPRESS

Use every letter tile below to complete the grid with familiar words.

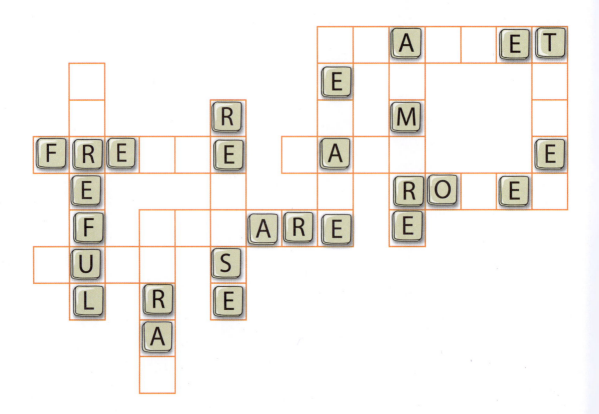

Answer on page 190.

Level   Words All Around!

DROP LETTERS

Use all three letter tiles to create four-letter words below. Each tile will be used once per word.

Answer on page 190.

Words All Around!

Level ★ ★

CRUNCHED LETTERS

Create three words by placing the letter tiles into the grid. Two tiles will be added to the three-letter sets given—one letter at the beginning and another at the end.

> Many dictionary definitions include the word's "etymology," which means the history of the word, if it originally came from another language, and how its meaning has changed over time.

Answer on page 190.

Level ★ Words All Around!

COME TOGETHER

Place each of the tile sets into the empty spaces below to create three nine-letter creatures. Each tile set is used only once.

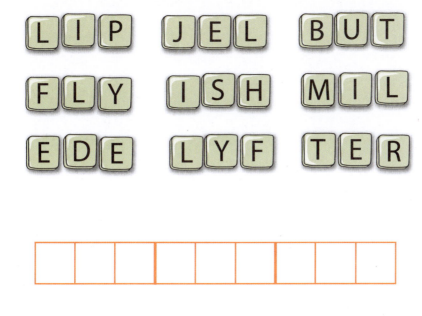

Words All Around! Level ★ ★ ★

ADD-A-LETTER

Rearrange the tiles from each word, adding one new tile from the bottom in order to form things related to ice hockey in the empty boxes. Each tile from the bottom of the page is used only once.

CUP → ☐☐☐☐

IRK → ☐☐☐☐

LAG → ☐☐☐☐

KITS → ☐☐☐☐☐

OHS → ☐☐☐☐

AGILE → ☐☐☐☐☐☐

RACES → ☐☐☐☐☐☐

T O O C E K N

hockey \'hä-kē\ *noun* : a game played on ice or in a field by two teams who try to drive a puck or ball through a goal by hitting it with a stick

Level ★ ★   Words All Around!

REPEAT REPEAT

Use the eight tiles given to complete each pair of words. Each pair will use the same four letter tiles in the same order.

Answer on page 191.

Words All Around! Level

TILE TIE-INS

Using the letter tiles below, complete the grid to reveal 12 types of fruit.

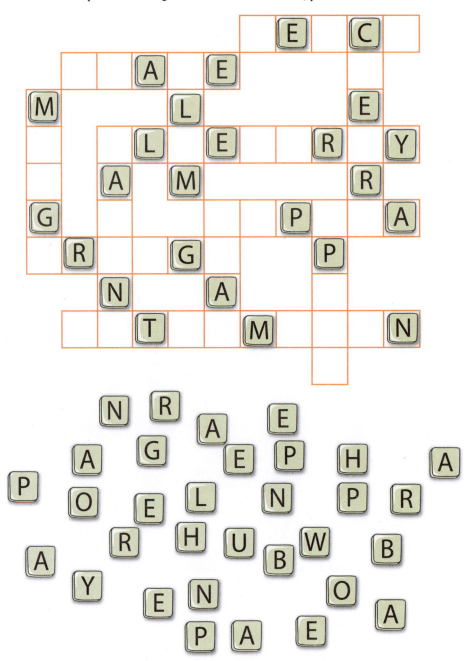

Answer on page 191.

Words All Around!

Level ★ ★ ★

SHUFFLE BOARD

Rearrange each of the letters in the words below to form new words. Place the new words into the grid. One letter has already been placed.

BEETS   FLITS

CABS   LEAF

FACES   SEATS

Lizard Linguistics

Don't let these puzzles discombobulate you and leave you feeling muzzy or addlepated. Did those weird words leave you feeling confused? Don't worry; they're all just synonyms of, or another way to say, confused!

Answer on page 191.

Words All Around! Level

REPEAT REPEAT

Use the eight tiles given to complete each pair of words. Each pair will use the same four letter tiles in the same order.

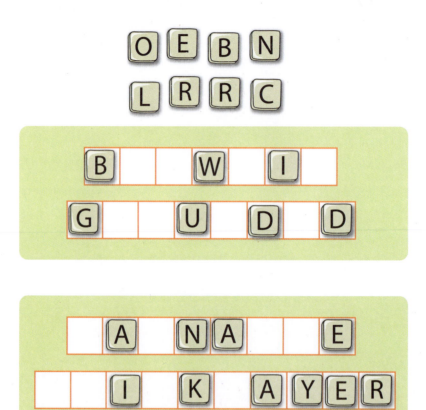

Level ★ ★ ★ Words All Around!

CHAIN WORDS

Place two letters in the middle squares that will complete one word and start another. For example, ER would complete FLI – ER – ROR.

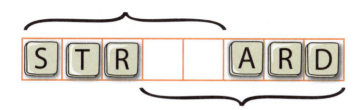

A "lipogram" is anything that's written without using a certain letter. Some people have written whole books this way! I haven't used the letter K yet, but that's an easy one. The most common letter in English is E—what can you say without using E? It's tricky, right?

Answer on page 191.

Words All Around! Level

THEME PARK

This "ride" has a theme, but we can't tell you what it is. Place all the words in the boxes below. Then read the word created in the outlined boxes, from top to bottom, to reveal the theme.

ACROBATS   PEANUTS
CLOWNS   RINGMASTER
MUSIC   TRAPEZE

funny

trapeze \tra-ˈpēz\ *noun* : a short horizontal bar hung from two parallel ropes and used by acrobats

Level ★ ★ ★ Words All Around!

DROP LETTERS

Use all three letter tiles to create four-letter words below.
Each tile will be used once in each word.

A G R

_ _ _ Y

D _ _ _

_ E _ _

_ _ _ E

_ _ N _

_ _ _ M

Words All Around! Level

WORD SWATTER

Create four common words using three letters each from the words below. Letters will be used more than once within the puzzle, but will only be used once per word.

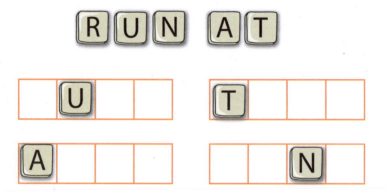

Lizard Linguistics

An "acronym" is a word that's made from the beginnings of other words. Some acronyms are easy to spot—like "FBI," which stands for "Federal Bureau of Investigation." But did you know that "scuba" is an acronym? It comes from "Self-Contained Underwater Breathing Apparatus." "Radar" and "laser" are acronyms too!

Answer on page 192.

Level ★ ★ ★   Words All Around!

ALPHABET EXPRESS

Use every letter tile below to complete the grid with common words.

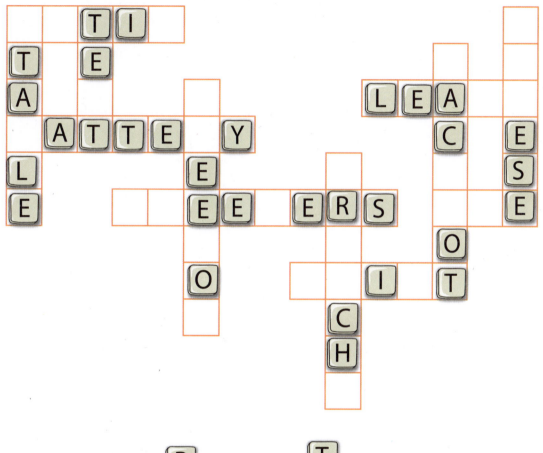

Answer on page 192.

Words All Around! Level

CROSSED OUT

Use the given tiles to spell a pair of related words that meet on the given letter.

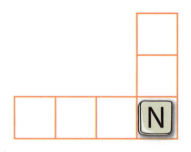

> One way to make new words is to squash existing words together. That's how we got "smog" (smoke + fog), "brunch" (breakfast + lunch), and "chortle" (chuckle + snort). When you combine words this way, it's called a "portmanteau"!

Answers

One Up (page 6)

S T R E A M E R S
A R M R E S T S
S M A R T E R
M A S T E R
S T E A M
S T E M
M E T

Add-a-Letter (page 7)

L I O N
T I G E R
B E A R
L L A M A
C A M E L
B I S O N

Word Swatter (page 8)
Answers may vary.

Crossed Out (page 9)

Shuffle Board (page 9)

Drop Letters (page 10)
bugs; busy; bush; cubs; snub; stub

Letter Gridlock (page 11)

Answers

Come Together (page 12)

V E N E Z U E L A

N I C A R A G U A

S I N G A P O R E

Theme Park (page 13)

```
    G H O S T S
    M A S K
    G O B L I N S
        L
        C O S T U M E
        W
  Z O M B I E S
    M A K E U P
    C A N D Y
```

Word Swatter (page 14)
Answers may vary.

S P O O N   N O T E S
T O O N S   A S P E N
P A S T E   S P E N T
S T O O P   S T O N E

Fitting Tiles (page 15)

L A B E L
A N I M E
S T A I N
T E S T S

Drop Letters (page 16)
stir; trip; dirt; riot; grit; trim

Repeat Repeat (page 17)

P O W E R F U L
T O W E L

M A C H I N E
S P A C I N G

Word Stickers (page 18)

B L A C K   N E A R
W H I T E   F A R

One Up (page 19)

S O U V E N I R S
V E R S I O N S
S E N I O R S
S E N S O R
S N O R E
N O S E
S O N

Answers

Alphabet Express (page 20)

Letter Gridlock (page 21)

Jumbled Up (page 21)

Word Swatter (page 22)
Answers may vary.

Shuffle Board (page 23)

Reword Rewind (page 23)
rats/star

Crunched Letters (page 24)
blame; clamp; llama

Come Together (page 25)

ASPARAGUS

SPAGHETTI

CASSEROLE

Answers

Tile Tie-Ins (page 26)

Shuffle Board (page 30)

Crossed Out (page 30)

Come Together (page 27)

Drop Letters (page 31)
boat; atom; toad; auto; oath; taco; atop

Fitting Tiles (page 28)

Add-a-Letter (page 32)

Reword Rewind (page 29)
mile/lime

Jumbled Up (page 29)

Drop Letters (page 33)
hint; into; thin; unit; tiny; twin

Answers

Word Swatter (page 34)
Answers may vary.

P	O	S	T		P	O	U	T
P	O	T	S		S	O	U	P
B	U	S	T		P	U	T	S
P	U	B	S		S	U	B	S
S	P	O	T		S	T	U	B

Reword Rewind (page 35)
tow/two

Jumbled Up (page 35)

N U M B E R

Drop Letters (page 36)
rain; ring; iron; ruin; grin; rind

Come Together (page 37)

L I T H U A N I A
I N D O N E S I A
S W A Z I L A N D

Fitting Tiles (page 38)

M A J O R
U S A G E
L I B R A
E A S E L

Word Stickers (page 39)

F L O W E R   S T A R E
F L O U R   S T A I R

Drop Letters (page 40)
risk; kids; sick; skip; inks; silk

Chain Words (page 41)

Z I P P E R S O N

Reword Rewind (page 41)
crate/trace

Word Stickers (page 42)

T I M E   B A N D
T H Y M E   B A N N E D

175

Answers

Theme Park (page 43)

Crunched Letters (page 44)
decal; pecan; recap

Fitting Tiles (page 45)

One Up (page 46)

Shuffle Board (page 47)

Add-a-Letter (page 48)

Letter Gridlock (page 49)

Piles of Tiles (page 50)

Answers

Drop Letters (page 51)
past; path; spat; pita; atop; pant

Shuffle Board (page 52)

```
    T
F E A R S
E   K   H
T   E   U
A S S E T
```

Plus One (page 53)
Answers may vary.

GENE   DASH
GLEE   HEAD
GEEK   HARD

Add-a-Letter (page 54)

BEANS
PEAS
SPINACH
BEETS
CORN
TURNIPS
ONIONS

Come Together (page 55)

ROCHESTER
MILWAUKEE
CLEVELAND

Add-a-Letter (page 56)

TEACHER
STUDY
TEST
RECESS
PAPER
TARDY
EXAM

Word Swatter (page 57)
Answers may vary.

GOAT   ATOM
MATE   TOGA
MEAT   GAME
MOAT   TAME

Piles of Tiles (page 58)

Answers

Tile Tie-Ins (page 59)

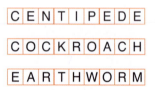

Come Together (page 60)

Piles of Tiles (page 61)

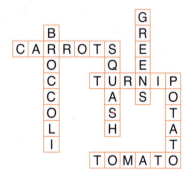

Drop Letters (page 62)
wild; dial; idle; slid; deli; idol

Plus One (page 63)

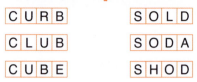

Theme Park (page 64)

Repeat Repeat (page 65)

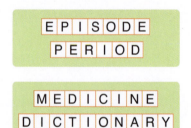

Chain Words (page 66)

Reword Rewind (page 66)
dad/add

Answers

Piles of Tiles (page 67)

Add-a-Letter (page 68)

FILE
PLANE
CHISEL
MALLET
HAMMER
CLAMP
SANDER

Tile Tie-Ins (page 69)

Come Together (page 70)

KOALABEAR
WOLVERINE
WOLFHOUND

Add-a-Letter (page 71)

BEANS
PEAS
SPINACH
BEETS
CORN
TURNIPS
ONIONS

Word Stickers (page 72)

SOFA
COUCH
BLANKET
QUILT

Add-a-Letter (page 73)

GOLF
POLO
TENNIS
SOCCER
RUGBY
ARCHERY

179

Answers

Tile Tie-Ins (page 74)

Word Swatter (page 78)
Answers may vary.

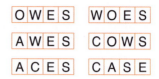

Reword Rewind (page 78)
lemon/melon

Letter Gridlock (page 75)

Letter Gridlock (page 79)

One Up (page 76)

Theme Park (page 80)

Drop Letters (page 81)
each; chew; echo; ache; chef; etch

Repeat Repeat (page 77)

180

Answers

Come Together (page 82)

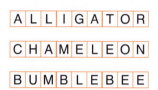

Theme Park (page 83)

Alphabet Express (page 84)

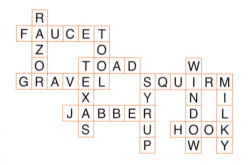

Jumbled Up (page 85)

Reword Rewind (page 85)
fear/fare

Plus One (page 86)

Tile Tie-Ins (page 87)

Shuffle Board (page 88)

Reword Rewind (page 88)
pans/naps/span

Crunched Letters (page 89)
fever; levee; seven

Chain Words (page 89)

Answers

Come Together (page 90)

NEW MEXICO
TENNESSEE
WISCONSIN

Piles of Tiles (page 91)

GREEN
YELLOW
ORANGE
INDIGO
VIOLET
BLUE
RED

Repeat Repeat (page 92)

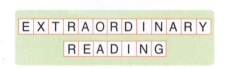

EXTRAORDINARY
READING

SNOWMAN
NOMADS

One Up (page 93)

RETALIATE
LITERATE
RETITLE
LITTER
LITER
TILE
LIE

Word Swatter (page 94)
Answers may vary.

RACED   ACRES
RACES   CARDS
CARED   DARES
CARES   CEDAR
SCARE   READS

Drop Letters (page 95)
also; logs; slow;
sold; soul; owls

Drop Letters (page 96)
cure; rule; true;
user; rude; urge

Word Swatter (page 97)
Answers may vary.

CATERS
CRATES
REACTS
TRACES

Answers

Chain Words (page 98)

Jumbled Up (page 98)

Fitting Tiles (page 99)

R	O	A	R	S
A	G	R	E	E
G	R	E	E	T
S	E	A	L	S

Theme Park (page 100)

Word Swatter (page 101)
Answers may vary.

| F | R | O | M | | F | O | R | E |
| F | O | R | M | | M | O | R | E |

Come Together (page 102)

C	O	C	K	A	T	O	O	S
A	L	B	A	T	R	O	S	S
S	A	N	D	P	I	P	E	R

Plus One (page 103)

B	A	T	H		A	C	E	S
B	A	I	T		F	A	C	E
B	R	A	T		A	C	H	E

Theme Park (page 104)

Shuffle Board (page 105)

	R	A	M	P
		O		
S	P	A	R	K
U			A	
B	U	G	L	E

183

Answers

Jumbled Up (page 106)

Shuffle Board (page 106)

Repeat Repeat (page 107)

Crunched Letters (page 108)

eager; pager; wages
eager; pages; wager

Jumbled Up (page 108)

Theme Park (page 109)

Come Together (page 110)

LOUISIANA

MINNESOTA

NEW JERSEY

Piles of Tiles (page 111)

Word Stickers (page 112)

Answers

Tile Tie-Ins (page 113)

Fitting Tiles (page 114)

Crunched Letters (page 115)
cough; gouge; tough

Jumbled Up (page 115)

Drop Letters (page 116)
wide; owed; weld; drew; awed; dewy

Plus One (page 117)

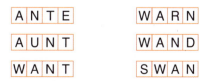

Piles of Tiles (page 118)

Chain Words (page 119)

Jumbled Up (page 119)

Drop Letters (page 120)
mail; palm; meal; lamb; malt; slam

Word Swatter (page 121)
Answers may vary.

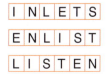

185

Answers

One Up (page 122)

Chain Words (page 123)

Crossed Out (page 123)

Jumbled Up (page 124)

Add-a-Letter (page 124)

Repeat Repeat (page 125)

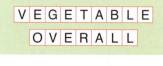

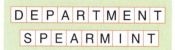

Crunched Letters (page 126)
daunt; haunt; sauna

Tile Tie-ins (page 127)

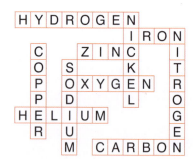

Plus One (page 128)

D	R	A	G		C	H	O	P
R	A	G	E		C	R	O	P
R	A	N	G		C	O	P	E

Come Together (page 129)

C	H	A	R	L	O	T	T	E
F	O	R	T	W	O	R	T	H
H	O	L	L	Y	W	O	O	D

Answers

Fitting Tiles (page 130)

A	C	O	R	N
R	A	D	I	O
C	R	O	S	S
S	P	R	E	E

Word Swatter (page 131)
Answers may vary.

L	A	P	S		P	A	L	S
S	L	A	P		A	L	P	S

Alphabet Express (page 132)

Shuffle Board (page 133)

Repeat Repeat (page 134)

Come Together (page 135)

A	R	G	E	N	T	I	N	A
A	U	S	T	R	A	L	I	A
C	O	S	T	A	R	I	C	A

Piles of Tiles (page 136)

Chain Words (page 137)

Answers

Add-a-Letter (page 137)

Theme Park (page 138)

Word Swatter (page 139)
Answers may vary.

Word Swatter (page 140)
Answers may vary.

TABLES	STABLE
TABLET	BATTLE
SETTLE	LATEST

Alphabet Express (page 141)

Tile Tie-Ins (page 142)

Crunched Letters (page 143)
cater; latex; water

Jumbled Up (page 143)

Answers

Add-a-Letter (page 144)

BRICK
CREAM
EDAM
GOAT
FETA
CHEDDAR
GOUDA

Repeat Repeat (page 145)

SHERIFF
SHELF

MACARONI
CROWNS

Word Stickers (page 146)

BLEW   CELLAR
BLUE   SELLER

Letter Gridlock (page 147)

```
      C
    P O P
  G O R E S
H A U N T E D
  S T R A W
    S O L
      W
```

Come Together (page 148)

BALDEAGLE
BLACKBIRD
GOLDFINCH

Jumbled Up (page 149)

NUMBER

Repeat Repeat (page 150)

KITCHEN
THICKEN

FLORIDA
FORCED

One Up (page 151)

BUTTERFLY
FLUTTERY
UTTERLY
TURTLE
UTTER
TRUE
RUT

Chain Words (page 152)

EARTHINK

Answers

Crossed Out (page 152)

Alphabet Express (page 156)
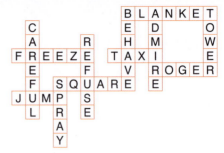

Plus One (page 153)

Drop Letters (page 157)
inch; coin; icon;
nice; chin; zinc

Add-a-Letter (page 154)

Crunched Letters (page 158)
kabob; labor; taboo

Come Together (page 159)

Come Together (page 155)

Answers

Add-a-Letter (page 160)

PUCK
RINK
GOAL
STICK
SHOT
GOALIE
CREASE

Repeat Repeat (page 161)

BANDANA
ABANDONED

NEIGHBOR
MIDNIGHT

Tile Tie-Ins (page 162)

Shuffle Board (page 163)

```
  F L E A
S I   S
C A F E S
A   T   E
B E S E T
```

Repeat Repeat (page 164)

BROWNIE
GROUNDED

BARNACLE
BRICKLAYER

Chain Words (page 165)

STRAWARD

Theme Park (page 166)

Answers

Drop Letters (page 167)
gray; drag; gear;
rage; rang; gram

Word Swatter (page 168)
Answers may vary.

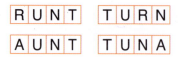

Alphabet Express (page 169)

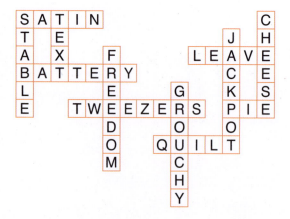

Crossed Out (page 170)